W9-CRQ-883

795.412 FOR
Fornatale, Peter Thomas
Poker aficionado

0509355

THE

POKER

AFICIONADO

Also by Pete Fornatale:

with Frank R. Scatoni
Six Secrets of Successful Bettors
Say Anything
Who Can It Be Now?

THE

POKER

AFICIONADO

AN ALL-IN COMPENDIUM OF
LORE & LEGEND, WIT & WISDOM,
TIPS & TECHNIQUES

♥ ♣ ♦ ♠

BY
PETE FORNATALE
WITH JONAH KERI

ILLUSTRATED AND
DESIGNED BY
PATRICK BRODERICK

BROADWAY BOOKS
NEW YORK

BROADWAY

PRINTED IN THE UNITED STATES OF AMERICA

BROADWAY BOOKS and its logo, a letter B bisected on
the diagonal, are trademarks of Random House, Inc.

Visit our website at www.broadwaybooks.com

First edition published 2005.

Book design and illustrations by Patrick Broderick

Library of Congress Cataloging-in-Publication Data
Fornatale, Peter.
    The poker aficionado : an all-in compendium of lore & legend, wit &
wisdom, tips & techniques / by Pete Fornatale with Jonah Keri ; illustrated
and designed by Patrick Broderick.
    p. cm.
ISBN 0-7679-2184-4 (alk. paper)
1. Poker--Miscellanea. I. Keri, Jonah. II. Title.

GV1253.F67 2005
795.412--dc22

                                                                    2005045739

10 9 8 7 6 5 4 3 2 1

"Last night I stayed up late playing poker with tarot cards. I got a full house and four people died."

—Steven Wright

For my mom

HOW TO USE THIS BOOK

THE POKER AFICIONADO is a one of a kind compendium of poker lore, facts, figures, nicknames, wit, tips and techniques. Will it make you a better player? Maybe yes, maybe no. But you are guaranteed to learn something. Whether that something is pre flop strategy in Texas Hold'em, the rules for Omaha/8 or the name of the guy who played the coach in *Teen Wolf* is entirely up to you.

You don't need to read this book cover to cover. The idea is to open to a random page and then take it from there. **There's a handy index of topics on page 197 if there's something particular you are looking for.**

Much of this book's material comes from outside sources, which are credited throughout the book and in the acknowledgments section at the back. It is highly recommended that you continue your poker education by exploring these sources at some point in the near future. But for now, let's shuffle up and deal.

SLIM-ISMS
The best sayings of Amarillo Slim

Someone who isn't too sharp

- *If it was raining soup, he'd be out in it with a fork.*
- *That boy is lighter than a June frost.*
- *He couldn't track an elephant in four feet of snow.*

Something of little value

- *That ain't worth nine settings of eggs.*

A conservative player in poker

- *Tighter than a nun's gadget.*

A person put in shock

- *He couldn't swallow boiled okra.*

A naïve person

- *He's as square as an apple box. He still thinks 69 is the new highway to Dallas.*

A close relationship

- *I'm closer to that boy than 19 is to 20.*

Major evidence that proves a point

- *That's stronger than Nellie's breath.*

A sucker who falls for a bad bet

- *Had taken the bait like a country hog after town slop.*
- *What he smelled cooking wasn't on the fire.*

An attractive woman

 ♦ *As pretty as a speckled pup under a red wagon.*

A big pot in poker or a lot of money

 ♦ *It had so many chips that a show dog couldn't jump over it.*
 ♦ *Enough hundred-dollar bills to burn up 40 wet mules.*

The chances of an underdog

 ♦ *Very seldom do the lambs slaughter the butcher.*

♦ ♦ ♦ ♦

SLIM ON SLIM

 ♦ I'm so skinny I look like the advance man for a famine.

 ♦ I can see a gnat's keester at a hundred yards.

 ♦ If there's anything I'll argue about, I'll either bet on it or shut up.

 ♦ I'm from a good town named Amarillo. The population has been 173,000 for the past 50 years, never varies – every time some woman gets pregnant, some man leaves town.

♦ ♦ ♦ ♦

PHILOSOPHICAL SLIM

 ♦ There's more horse's asses than there are horses.

 ♦ You can shear a sheep many a time, but you can skin 'em only once.

 ♦ You can't always win. Sometimes they milk me like a Rocky Mountain goat. My titties get so sore I can't button my shirt.

 ♦ Would I like my son to be a professional making a living as a gambler? No, he'd be better off getting him a driver's license and go to driving a dump truck.

PHIL HELLMUTH, JR.'S, "ANIMAL TYPES"

Phil Hellmuth, Jr., has won nine bracelets at the World Series of Poker. He's one of the best all-around players in the game today. Phil's books, Play Poker Like the Pros *and* Bad Beats and Lucky Draws, *are essential additions to any poker library. Here he describes common poker foes by picturing them as different animal types.*

THE MOUSE: The mouse is extremely conservative. He plays only super-strong hands and rarely bluffs. To him, a pair of eights is a weak hand. He hardly ever raises when someone else has bet and when he does, it's best to just get out of his way.

THE LION: The lion is also a fairly tight player but he plays with more imagination and style than the mouse. He'll play a wider array of hands and has excellent timing when it comes to bluffing and knowing when he's being bluffed. You could do worse than to play like him.

THE JACKAL: The jackal is what many players would call a "maniac." He's loose and unpredictable and liable to have huge swings in his chip stack since he plays so many hands so aggressively. Be careful of the jackal because there is some method to his madness. When he's timing his raises well and catching good cards, he's going to win a ton of money. But he can just as easily throw away his entire stack.

THE ELEPHANT: The elephant is a different type of loose player than the jackal. He's a "calling station": he never folds when he's supposed to, so don't bother bluffing him, ever, because he won't believe you anyway. He's a guy that most players will do very well against – except the jackal, who continually tries to bluff against him.

THE EAGLE: A rare bird indeed, the eagle is one of the top 100 poker players in the world, and you might not ever sit across from him. You'll find him wherever high-stakes poker is played.

PHIL HELLMUTH, JR., ON WHEN TO FOLD POCKET ACES BEFORE THE FLOP

Now, mind you, despite a recent tongue-in-cheek example I wrote about in my column, this won't come up too often. But there is an example where it could happen and would absolutely be the right play. Let's say you're in a super-satellite tournament and you have 30% of the chips. The top eight players win seats for the World Series of Poker and there are nine players remaining. A player with more chips than you moves all-in. This is a time where it would be correct to fold pocket aces.

After all, the top eight players all get paid the same in a super-satellite. Why risk getting eliminated when you're only a four-and-a-half to one favorite or less? Your other option – to fold and wait for someone else to go broke – is the right play here. It just goes to show you, never say never in poker!

FAMOUS POKER MOVIES

1. CALIFORNIA SPLIT: A pair of degenerate horse players/poker players get in a tough spot and end up in a game in Reno with it all on the line. You've got to love any movie that was partially filmed at Santa Anita and features a cameo by Amarillo Slim. Robert Altman (*MASH*, *Nashville*, *The Player*) directed and George Segal and Elliot Gould (Monica and Ross's dad on *Friends* for those of you born post-1980) starred.

2. HONEYMOON IN VEGAS: Nothing says "I love you" like losing your fiancée in a card game in Vegas. Yeah, it was fixed but try telling that to Sarah Jessica Parker. A really great movie, particularly the card scene that features Max's dad from *Rushmore*, Jerry "The Shark" Tarkanian, and an Asian Elvis impersonator. This film contains some of Jimmy Caan's best work. Seriously.

3. MY LITTLE CHICKADEE: Perhaps the first film to prominently feature poker. You might not think it now, but six decades ago the screen pairing of Mae West and W.C. Fields was a big deal. Stranger still, the two apparently wrote the screenplay together for this sucker. Though that sounds about as likely as being dealt a royal straight flush.

4. THE CINCINNATI KID: This one's a classic. Great cast, cool plot. And you get to see what Phil Gordon calls "the greatest bad beat in the history of poker cinema." Steve McQueen gives his typical awesome performance and Edward G. Robinson is truly "the man."

5. A BIG HAND FOR THE LITTLE LADY: Long before Annie Duke, there was a woman kicking ass at the poker table. But first she had to learn to play. This one's a very goofy comedy western. Look for Burgess Meredith (the Penguin, Rocky's manager) sitting at the table.

6. COOL HAND LUKE: One guess where Paul Newman's character got his nickname. If you said "the poker table," you got it right. Even more impressive than Luke's prowess at the table, however, is his ability to eat hard-boiled eggs.

7. ROUNDERS: A movie that might have set box office records had it been released just a few years later, one could argue that this picture's release helped launch the poker boom and created thousands of wanna-be Mike McDermott's. In other words, the film that launched millions of dollars worth of dead money. The film's a must-see, and features John Malkovich doing everything short of chewing on the scenery as Matt Damon's foil.

8. McCABE AND MRS. MILLER: Altman again. You think he likes cards? This time we're in the old West, but this isn't like any old West you've seen before. Warren Beatty is awesome as McCabe, a card hustling entrepreneur who has a background as a gunfighter and a killer – or does he?

ENTERING THE WSOP:
NO GUTS, NO GLORY

The simplest way to enter the annual World Series of
Poker (WSOP) is to visit Binion's Horseshoe in downtown Las Vegas and pay $10,000. Do that and your
name is posted to the board and you've got a seat at
the Main Event.

Harrah's has now created a WSOP
Circuit, with five tournaments feeding qualifying players into the Main
Event based on a points system,
transforming the month-long poker
event into a year-round sport. Buy-
ins for these tournaments range from
$500 to $10,000. While there are
even more affordable options to get a
seat at the main event, bear in mind
that as the entry fees decrease, the
number of opponents you'll face
increases proportionally – meaning it's going to be
tougher to qualify.

> Not willing
> to leave your
> house in pur-
> suit of your
> seat at the
> WSOP tables?
> No problemo.
> You still have
> a shot at
> the glory.

There are also a number of other tournaments that will
allow you to qualify for the WSOP, known as satellites.
These are usually one-table affairs with a buy-in of
around $1,000 (plus the "juice" which is typically
about $60), where the winner goes on to the big dance.
There are also prequalifying events known as super-
satellites, which will typically cost about $200 but you'll
have to beat a lot more opponents.

Not willing to leave your house in pursuit of your seat
at the WSOP tables? No problemo. You still have a
shot at the glory à la Chris Moneymaker (2003) and
Greg Raymer (2004). Again, the cheaper the buy-in,

the bigger the field. Moneymaker entered an Internet super-satellite for $39 and Raymer's online buy-in was still only $160. Their success just goes to show that

players can find myriad ways to win a WSOP seat with only an Internet connection and a little luck. Internet satellites and super-satellites can be found in online poker rooms and are structured just like the land-based competitions, without all the staring.

♥ ♦ ♣ ♠

WALKING BACK TO HOUSTON

Poker author/champion Barry Greenstein tells a story on his website about one of the more unusual hand nicknames, Walking Back to Houston. According to Greenstein, when he and T.J. Cloutier first played Hold'em together, they talked about the differences between the way the game was played in Houston and Dallas (Barry played in Houston and T.J. played more in Dallas). Barry then moved in on another player with ace-king (A-K). The other guy, who had queen-queen (Q-Q), called. Barry went on to win the race and the hand. T.J. said, "I can see you learned to play in Houston. Those Houston players would come to Dallas and play that ace-king, but they'd always end up against a pair of aces. That's why we call that hand 'Walking Back to Houston.'"

TIPPING

I don't tip because society says I have to. Alright, I tip when somebody really deserves a tip. If they put forth an effort, I'll give them something extra. But I mean, this tipping automatically, that's for the birds. As far as I'm concerned they're just doing their job.

–Mr. Pink (Steve Buscemi) in *Reservoir Dogs*

Here's a nickel's worth of free advice: when you're playing in a cardroom, make sure to tip your dealer. We've all heard arguments similar to the above against tipping. But as in the case of Mr. Pink, the person making the argument is usually a sociopath. Do not follow that lead. The average dealer makes about $6/hour for doing a job that's a lot harder than it looks. When you take down a pot, throw them a buck. When you take down a big pot, throw them a few bucks. It's not necessarily going to increase your bottom line but it will be good for your karma. You don't want to end up like Mr. Pink.

NAMES FOR A PAIR OF QUEENS:	NAMES FOR A 10/4:	NAMES FOR A PAIR OF 8s:
Ladies	Broderick Crawford	Pocket Snowmen
Jailhouse Rock	Over and Out	Two Fat Ladies
Sigfried and Roy	Roger That	Dawg Balls
Four Tits	The Good Buddy	Racetracks

RANK OF HANDS

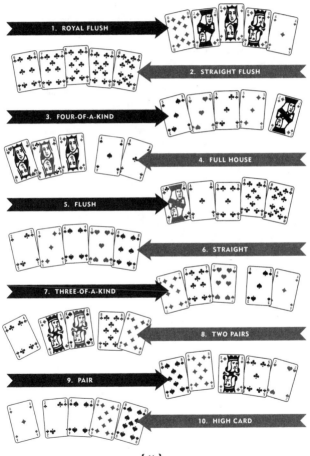

1. ROYAL FLUSH
2. STRAIGHT FLUSH
3. FOUR-OF-A-KIND
4. FULL HOUSE
5. FLUSH
6. STRAIGHT
7. THREE-OF-A-KIND
8. TWO PAIRS
9. PAIR
10. HIGH CARD

It's fitting that the biggest event of the poker universe started as a glorified home game between old buddies.

Several years after relocating to Las Vegas from Texas, Benny Binion accepted an invitation from his old friend Tom Moore to attend the "Texas Gambler's Reunion" in 1969. The premise was to gather several famous Texas road gamblers – "Texas Dolly" Doyle Brunson, Amarillo Slim Preston, Jack "Treetop" Straus and others – to play in a poker tournament. Moore had bought the Holiday Hotel in Reno, and he wanted an event that could attract a bit of attention for its grand reopening.

> Would people really come out to watch a bunch of cowboys play poker?

It was an interesting, if risky, gambit. Poker was mostly the province of pool halls, bar back rooms and seedy clubs in those days, with Texans making up most of the game's few heavy hitters. Texas Hold'em, the game favored by many of poker's heavyweights, was little known to players and watchers outside Texas. A vaunted showgirls' cabaret or a headliner lounge singer would have seemed a better bet to bring business to the Holiday. Would people really come out to watch a bunch of cowboys play poker?

To many people's surprise, the event was a hit, drawing a large crowd. A Texan himself and a poker aficionado going way back, Binion suddenly saw an opportunity. If done right, Binion realized he could open up the game of poker to a wider audience. This wasn't some act of altruism or an offering to the poker gods. A shrewd businessman, Binion's primary motivation was to make money. If Binion could replicate the Texas Gambler's Reunion with more players and more cash at stake, he felt he could bring more people into Binion's Horseshoe casino in downtown Las Vegas to spend money.

Though the players liked the idea, most of Binion's family opposed it. Since players battle each other and not the casino, the house can only collect the rake – a small predetermined sum of money – on each pot. Poker was long known as a far less profitable game for casinos than slot machines or other table games: A poker room's earnings compared to an area of slots that big is about 10-to-1 in favor of the slots. Floor space was too valuable to waste on a game where the casino could only collect a small fee for running the game. But Binion's vision had been forged: Make the tournament a loss leader for the casino, and he could rake in the bucks getting more players and more watchers in to stay the weekend and blow their dollars at the Horseshoe.

The next year, Binion moved to make his vision a reality, launching "The World Series of Poker." Brought together in a small room normally reserved for baccarat, Binion lured players to the Horseshoe to play five variations of poker. The guest list included many of the players at the previous year's event at the Holiday, as well as Johnny Moss, who cemented his reputation as the best poker player in the world when his fellow players voted him the best all-around player at the end of the event. (The next segment on WSOP history starts on page 24.)

BETTING STRUCTURES

There are four different ways that poker betting limits can be set up.

Fixed-limit: A fixed-limit set-up is the one you'll see in most cardrooms. In a $1-$2 Limit Hold'em game, you can only bet in $1 increments on the first two betting rounds and $2 on the last two betting rounds. With home games that use fixed limit, it's common that the limit on the last round will increase a third time – maybe the limits will be $1, $2, $3 on the end.

Spread-limit: This is the most common betting structure in home game poker, with any amount between the minimum and maximum allowed to be made at any time. Casinos and cardrooms also offer spread-limit games but note that in those places, after the first bet all subsequent raises must be made at that level or higher. If Player A bets $5, Player B cannot then raise $1 – he must raise at least $5 (or he can call or fold).

Pot-limit: The idea of pot-limit is that you can bet or raise any amount up to the size of the pot. Pot-limit can lead to some serious scores without having to risk your entire bankroll at once like you must in no limit. That said, pot-limit is not a game for a rank amateur.

No-limit: As seen on TV! No-limit lets you bet or raise all your money at one time. It's an extremely exciting version of the game but it's not recommended for beginners unless you're playing in a tournament where the buy-in is way within the number of chips you're OK losing in one sitting.

RAISE LIMITS

It is standard practice in home games to allow a maximum of three raises per round of betting; in Las Vegas and in many cardrooms, four raises per round are permissible. It's also common that on the final betting round, when it comes down to just two players (a situation called "heads up"), an unlimited amount of raises are allowed.

♥ ♦ ♦ ♠

THE RULES FOR FIVE-CARD DRAW

Woefully out of fashion though it may be, Five-Card Draw is still the first game many people ever learned (people born before 1985 anyway).

First, there's an ante. Five facedown cards are dealt to each player. The first round of betting commences with the player to the dealer's left. He can either check or bet. Subsequent players can still check (if no one has bet) or call (match a previous bet), raise (bet a larger amount that the original bettor will have to call) or fold (exit the hand). Then, in turn, the players can choose to draw up to three new cards, discarding an equal amount of their old ones into the center of the table, called the muck. There's a school of thought that allows you to draw four cards to an ace, but this is silly for a variety of reasons and is generally frowned upon by the more discerning home players.

After all remaining players have drawn, there is a final round of betting that proceeds very much like the first. When the last bet is called, there is a showdown where the cards are revealed – the last raise from the final round of betting shows first.

THE RULES FOR SEVEN-CARD STUD

Every player antes. Then the dealer doles out two down cards (also called hole cards) and one face up card (also called the door card). A round of betting commences (called third street). Another upcard and round of betting (called fourth street) follows. The same process occurs for fifth street and sixth street. The final card is dealt face down and is known as seventh street, but as with the final card in Hold'em, it can also be called the river.

After all the players have seven cards, the player making the best five card hand wins.

It's typical that the betting maximums will increase as the game progresses. Perhaps the maximum bet will be $5 through fourth street and then increase to $10 for the remainder. Sometimes a larger bet on fourth street is allowed if the player has a pair showing.

Seven-Stud can be played with up to eight players, though with eight it is theoretically possible that you might run out of cards. If that ever looks like it might happen, instead of dealing the river card face down, the dealer should flip a card face up on the table and make that a community card for the remaining players.

♥ ♣ ♦ ♠

IMPORTANT DIFFERENCES BETWEEN SEVEN-STUD AT HOME AND IN A CARD ROOM

At home, the first round of betting on third street is traditionally done by the high card showing; that is, any player with an ace will bet first, followed by K, Q, etc., all down the line. If there are two of the same high card showing, the high card closest to the left of the dealer opens the betting.

In a cardroom, there is usually a forced bet, also called the bring in, that must be made by the player with the lowest card showing. If there are two low cards of equal value, you decide who bets first by suit rank (low to high: spades, hearts, diamonds, clubs).

What's the reason for this difference? In casino games, where players typically play a lot tighter, the bring in forces the action and helps build the pot, kind of like the blinds in Hold'em. In home games, there are usually a lot more calls and building the pot isn't a problem so the bring in can be dispensed with.

♥ ♠ ♦

THE BEST STARTING HANDS IN SEVEN-CARD STUD

1. Three-of-a-kind, from aces on down to twos (this is known as being "rolled up," as in, "I had rolled up aces.")

2. A pair, from aces on down to twos

3. Three cards to a flush

4. Three cards to a straight

AMARILLO SLIM ON HIS ROLE IN KENNY ROGERS' SUCCESS WITH "THE GAMBLER"

I had played poker a few times with Kenny Rogers, who was born in 1938 in Houston, Texas, and we got to be pretty good buddies over the years. So one day in 1978, Kenny approached Steve (Wynn) and me about a song he was working on about gambling. Figuring that the best place to help him get a feel for the lyrics – which were written by Bud Schlitz – would be in a cardroom, we sat down right in the poker room at the Golden Nugget and talked about "The Gambler." Steve and I played poker and Kenny would watch us and ask us questions: "What's this about Hold'em?"

"Well, how does the song go?" I asked.

"The chorus starts with," Kenny said, breaking into song, "'You got to know when to hold 'em and know when to fold 'em.'"

"Well that's the truth," I said. "But you also got to know when to quit."

So then Kenny sang, "'You got to know when to walk away and know when to run.'"

It went back and forth like that for a while and gosh darn I thought it was the greatest song I ever heard. And on December 23 of that year, Kenny hit the charts with "The Gambler," which was a number-one country hit, and two years later, starred in his own TV movie based on the smash hit record. To this day, Kenny and I are good friends. He even takes my grandbaby backstage whenever he has a concert in Houston. During the show, he'll introduce Heather to the audience from the stage as "Amarillo Slim's granddaughter."

GRATEFUL DEAD
LYRICS ABOUT POKER

- "Watch each card you play and play it slow," from "Deal"

- "I can tell the queen of diamonds by the way she shine," from "Loser"

- "Sittin' plush with a royal flush, aces back to back," from "Ramble On Rose"

- "Sometime – the cards ain't worth a dime if you don't lay 'em down," from "Truckin'"

- "She was too pat to open and too cool to bluff," from "Scarlet Begonias"

THE BEST POKER SONGS

4. BOB SEGER, "STILL THE SAME" Seger used poker as a metaphor to describe the lifestyles of the people that he met when he moved to Hollywood from Detroit. On its surface, though, it's very much about poker – there are references in every verse.

3. JERRY REED, "UPTOWN POKER CLUB" Country star Reed had a starring role in the Smokey and the Bandit series and he penned one of the great poker story songs of all time – about a habitually losing player who takes matters into his own hands.

2. MOTÖRHEAD, "ACE OF SPADES" Full of dark poker imagery, "Ace of Spades" has to be up at the top of any list of great poker songs regardless of how you feel about metal and Lemmy's hoarse bark of a voice. Plus, one of the song's co-writers, "Fast Eddie" Clarke, has a great name for a card player.

1. KENNY ROGERS, "THE GAMBLER" (see pg. 18)

GOING LIGHT

In home poker, if a player is low on chips and can't cover his bets, it's customary to allow him or her to "go light" and borrow chips from the pot that will be paid back immediately after the hand.

In a cardroom, however, there is no going light. They play what is called table stakes – meaning you can only bet what you have in front of you. If you don't have enough chips to cover, you can't get more until the hand is over. Depending on the house rules, you might be able to play a bill if it's a hundred, but that's usually it. If you do opt to go all-in when you have the option of going light, it will probably cost you a lot of money in the long run. Let's say you've got pocket aces in Hold'em and only $5 in chips. You can go all-in with your $5 and if two other players call your bet, you're only playing for the blinds and that $15. Your opponents can continue betting, with their money going into a side pot. If you win, you win that main pot, and the second hand high will take the side pot.

> If you opt to go all-in when you have the option of going light, it will probably cost you a lot of money in the long run.

Online poker brings up another issue. Some players will win a big pot, withdraw from the game, then reappear with less cash, having "squirreled" away the money they just won. They think it's an advantage to be able to go all-in and see the remaining cards at a seeming discount – but over the long run this will lose a good player far more money than it will save because when you win, you'll win a lot less than if you had the cash to cover your bets.

WHAT YOU NEED TO KNOW BEFORE
YOU START A HOME POKER GAME

John Vorhaus is one of the foremost experts on home poker in America. His book, Poker Night *(St. Martin's 2004), is the Hoyle of home poker and contains a wealth of information on how to have a great home game that will prepare you for play in the cardroom and beyond. Here are his keys to keep players coming back to your home game.*

1. Set an appropriate gulp limit. This is the amount of money that most players in your game will think twice about. Set it too low and it feels like there's nothing at stake. Set it too high and someone's going to head home never wanting to come back. The gulp limit should be right about what a player would feel OK losing for an evening of entertainment.

2. Establish betting limits. Maybe you want to start off with limits of $1, $2, with $3 allowed on the last round of betting. Your betting limits should give you a good idea of what your buy-in should be, usually 25 to 30 times the size of your big bet. So in this case, each player will start with $75 in chips. If your groups' gulp limit is around $75, these stakes should work perfectly for you. If not, you should lower or raise accordingly.

3. The spread. New players might want to have an idea of what the spread in your game is – that is, how much money can they expect to win or lose in any given evening. A spread of 100 times plus or minus the big bet is theoretically possible (in this case +300/-300) but that's a pretty extreme example. Still, if the idea of losing $300 terrifies you, you should probably be hosting a lower stakes game.

4. You need to have a (preferably written) set of house rules. See page 185 for an example that you can feel free to steal for your own personal use.

5. You need a reliable group of six or seven people. If someone in your group flakes out, feel free to give first dibs next time to someone for whom the game is more of a priority.

6. Consider investing in high-end clay chips and/or a decent poker table (or at least table top).

7. You need to establish if yours is a smoking game or a non-smoking game.

8. Booze. My advice: give your friends as much as they'll drink but you stay away from the stuff, at least until the game is over.

9. Food. It's entirely appropriate to provide food, especially if it's an after-work game and the other players won't have eaten (if it's later, snacks will do). It is recommended that you collect an extra $5 or $10 at the buy-in to put towards food or beer or new cards or any other game-related expenses.

10. If a situation comes up that isn't covered by the house rules, the host makes the call and his/her word is final. Note to the host: if you can't be right, be loud.

Though the newly-branded event met with some modest success, Binion knew something wasn't quite right. After gathering the world's best poker players to battle for days in the same room, it seemed anticlimactic to simply stage a vote and hand out a trophy. A big part of what made poker so great was the gunslinger mentality – one man and his own fortune pitted against the wits and bankrolls of a table full of other desperadoes.

"How many people would watch the Kentucky Derby if a bunch of horses ran around the track and then all the jockeys voted on the winner?" Amarillo Slim Preston said at the time. "All the times that poker had been played with a big crowd – like when Johnny Moss played Nick the Greek – it had been a freezeout. There wasn't any drama in seeing the chips pass back and forth; what got people excited was seeing a person get eliminated."

The best way to make the World Series worthy of its name, Preston, Binion and others realized, was to tap into the gunslinger mentality. Put real money on the line in a winner-take-all format, with combatants using the rough-and-tumble game of No-Limit Texas Hold'em as the big stage. Flash the almighty green out there, and more of the game's best would surely show up to play. More importantly, more publicity and more spectators would follow, bringing more money to Binion and his casino. That was the hope, anyway.

The inaugural winner-take-all freezeout format of the World Series didn't bring that pot of gold. Far from it:

Only six people paid the $5,000 entry fee to enter the tournament. With all the suspense of trip-aces prevailing against a pair of deuces after the flop, Moss disposed of his five opponents to take home the money. The prize pool was doubled the next year. Yet despite the raised stakes, only two more people joined the fray, as eight players did battle in 1972. The next year saw the tournament expand to 13 players, prompting Binion to gush: "It's liable to get up to 50, might get up to be more than that."

Binion's optimism was born not only of the World Series' Main Event, as it was called. By 1973, the Horseshoe played host to championship events for Texas Hold'em, Seven-Card Razz, Deuce to Seven Draw and Seven-Card Stud. Side games started breaking out throughout the casino, drawing more spectators. Many of the side games rivaled the Main Event for the amount of cash on the line – there was action everywhere, and people started getting more interested.

> How many people would watch the Kentucky Derby if a bunch of horses ran around the track and then all the jockeys voted on the winner?

Still, the early years of the World Series were dominated by the old guard. Preston, Brunson, Puggy Pearson, Sailor Roberts and Moss took turns passing the grand prize around from 1971 to 1977. It was high-quality poker, to be sure, but remained largely a game appreciated by die-hards, with little appeal to broad audiences. But that was about to change. (The next segment on WSOP history starts on page 90.)

BEST POKER HOME GAMES

For maximum home-game entertainment, it's hard to beat a rollicking Hold'em tournament. But you can play Hold'em or stud anywhere. If you're looking for fun, intricate games you won't find at any casino, look no further.

✹ ANACONDA ✹

How to play: Deal seven cards, and everybody antes. Each player then passes three cards to his left, then another three-card pass to the left. Another two cards are then passed to the right, and each player then discards two cards, leaving a five-card poker hand. At this point each player puts his cards in whatever order he chooses, face down. Everyone then starts flipping their cards over, one at a time. After each player flips a card, there's a round of betting. The hand ends at the last round of betting, just before the last card is turned.

Quick tip: The chaotic nature of Anaconda, including the multiple passes and using the best five cards to make your hand, means that straights, flushes, and full houses are fairly common.

✹ INDIAN POKER ✹

How to play: One of the silliest poker games, Indian Poker is typically played at parties or when beer has surpassed poker as the goal of the evening – it's still good for some fun once in a while. There's virtually no limit to the amount of players, but usually six to 10 work best. Ace is high card. Each player antes. Using one deck of cards, the dealer deals a card, face down, to each player around the table. The players then place the cards on their foreheads with one hand, so all players except themselves can see what they're playing with. The card stays held there until the end of the round. If a player looks at their own card, they're out of the round, and out their ante. One by one, starting with the dealer, each player bets or folds. Decisions are based on what a player believes their unseen card is compared to others' seen cards. Once all bets are in, everyone sees their hand. High card takes the pot.

Quick tip: This game can actually have some useful application to more serious poker. In between chuckling at how ridiculous everyone else looks, most players will give away what you have slapped on your forehead by their facial expression. Ideally you'll gain a better understanding of how to read tells and eventually learn to play your ace or fold your deuce based on how others react to you. The game also teaches you to adopt a poker face of your own. Can you keep a straight face when your friend with a three on his noggin keeps raising?

✄ GUTS ✄

How to play: Deal three cards each. Best hands are as follows: three of a kind, pair, high card (flushes and straights forbidden). All players then hold their cards with their palms facing downward. The dealer then calls out "1-2-3-guts!" On "guts!" you either drop your cards to fold or hold on to stay in. If one person stays in, he wins the pot, game over. If more than one person stays in, the winner takes the pot, the loser(s) match(es) what was in the pot, and the game continues.

Quick tip: This game can get very expensive, so if you don't want players to blow their bankroll on this game, consider instituting a maximum dollar amount, time or hand limit.

Guts variations: "Counting Guts" is a highest-points-wins game. Ante up, everyone gets three cards, two face down, one face up. The card values go 2=2, 3=3, etc.... 10=10, J=11, Q=12, K=13, A=14. One round of betting, then each player goes around and can exchange one card (or they can opt not to). No matter which card you switch – whether it's face up or not – you get one face up in return, which provides a disadvantage, as the other players now know more about your hand. Then comes another betting round, followed by the "1-2-3-guts!" drop-or-hold count. The game stops if one person stays in, or goes on if more than one does. As with regular Guts, loser(s) must match the pot, and there's potential for huge pots.

"3-8-1," where everyone gets three cards, 8s are wild. Call "1-2-3 guts!," same rules of stay to play apply. After that you can opt to draw one card and discard one to try and improve your hand. Another pot-matching game, "3-8-1" ends when only one person stays in, but with a twist: He must then beat the hand forged by the top three cards on the deck, known as the "ghost hand." If the ghost hand wins, he must match the pot and the game continues.

SEVEN-CARD STUD SPIN-OFFS: ✹ BLACK CHICAGO ✹

How to play: Usually played as a seven-card stud game, though Black Chicago can also be played as a five-card draw. Typically a split-pot game, the object is to assemble the best poker hand (no wild cards) and also have the highest spade in the hole. Everyone is dealt two cards face down and one face up, then the betting starts. Betting continues after every subsequent round, with four cards total being dealt face up, the last one face down. You can win the entire pot if you win both the best-hand and highest-spade-down battles.

Quick tip: Bet like mad if you've got the ace of spades, as it's the equivalent of having the nuts in Hold'em. If you've got a middling poker hand and no significant spade down, fold quickly.

Bonus Black Chicago game: In this version, the game continues until someone gets both the best poker hand and the highest spade in the hole. If that doesn't occur in the first game, everyone except those who have folded must ante again and play a new hand. The lower number of players makes it easier to win with a lower spade – aggression begins to get increasingly rewarded.

SEVEN-CARD STUD SPIN-OFFS:
❧ FOLLOW THE QUEEN ❧

How to play: A wild game with sudden swings, Follow the Queen starts as a game of regular Seven-Card Stud: Everyone gets dealt two cards down, one up, followed by a round of betting and more betting after every subsequent round. The twist comes when a queen is dealt face up to any player. At that point, the next card dealt face up becomes wild for all. If or when other queens come face up, the wild card changes and the prior wild card ceases to be wild. If the last up card is a queen, then there are no wild cards. In some versions, if the last up card is a queen, then queens are wild.

Quick tip: Players have the option on the last card of taking their card face up or face down. Generally you'd prefer face down, since if a queen hits your hand, only the player after you is assured of getting a wild card. It's a smart strategy, however, if you have a strong natural hand while another player has a strong hand based mostly on wild cards.

BUSINESS AND POKER

In his book, *The Poker MBA*, Greg Dinkin does a great job explaining how the skills required to succeed in poker aren't useless in the outside world. On the contrary, a champion poker player's skill set is very much the same as that of a successful CEO:

- They are adept at reading others and seeing things from another's perspective

- They are able to balance risk and reward

- They are disciplined enough to handle adversity and recover from a loss

- They are good enough actors to "fake it" and win – they can bluff

▼ ♦ ♦ ♦

THE BUSINESS EQUIVALENTS OF POKER LINGO

POKER LINGO	EXPLANATION	BUSINESS EQUIVALENT
All-in	When a player puts his last chips in a pot.	Fully leveraged.
Cold Deck	When a new deck is put into a game in order to cheat a player.	Receiving payment in cash from an IRS informer.

POKER LINGO	EXPLANATION	BUSINESS EQUIVALENT
Floorman	The person in charge of a poker game in a casino.	The office manager.
Going Light	Not having enough chips to cover your bets.	Not paying the employees on Friday.
Houseman	The person in charge of a private poker game.	Your spouse.
Live One	A bad player.	A customer who pays retail.
The Pit	The "pit" refers to games of chance in the casino such as blackjack, craps, roulette and slots. In the long run, it's impossible to win in the pit, and could be better described as the "money pit."	Day trading.
Rail	The outside of a poker game. Also, a bystander, typically broke, who stands on the rail. "Railbirds" are people who hang around poker casinos.	Management consultants.
Stuck	When a player is stuck, he or she is losing.	Chapter 11.
Vig	Also called the "rake" – the amount of money taken out for the house.	Overhead.

For more on poker and business, check out
http://www.thepokermba.com

THE RULES FOR SEVEN-CARD STUD HIGH-LOW SPLIT

This is one of the best games in home poker. It's definitely a real poker game, and one that will satisfy the folks in your game who hate wild cards and goofy home poker derivatives. But there's also a lot of betting and a wide variety of playable starting hands, which will please the guy who calls out Anaconda all the time. If these rules seem a bit complicated, just read them over again because they're really not, especially if you're playing cards speak. Stick with it and Seven-Card Stud High-Low Split is sure to become a staple of your home poker play.

Before you start, you must decide if you're playing with a qualified low (pg. 95) or not.

You also must decide if you're playing cards speak, bet declare, or bet declare bet. More on those choices below.

The early stages of the game play out exactly like the normal Seven-Stud. You are dealt two hole cards and a face up or "door" card and the betting starts from there. Then there are three additional up cards dealt one at a time, each followed by a round of betting. The final card is dealt face down. As in regular Seven-Stud, the best five-card hand wins. But in high-low, you can use two different sets of five cards to make two different hands.

For example:

Your best low hand is the A-2-3-4-6 and your best high hand is the trip sixes.

Your best low hand is the A-3-4-6-7 and your best high is an ace-high flush.

❦

DETERMINING THE WINNER

This is where it gets interesting. You have a few options.

CARDS SPEAK: If you're playing cards speak, the players who are still in simply flip over their cards and the player with the best high hand takes half the pot and the person with the best low hand takes the other half. Of course, as in the example above, it's possible one player will win both and thus scoop the pot – that is, win the whole enchilada.

BET DECLARE: With bet declare it's a bit more complicated. You must indicate before the showdown which way you're going. Typically, holding no chip in your hand means you're going low. Holding one chip means you're looking to win the high. And if you want to go for both, also called going pig, you put two chips in your hand. Now if you want to be a pig and go both, you've got to win both. If the pig loses, the pot is split between the players with the next highest and/or lowest hands.

BET DECLARE BET: In bet declare bet, after the declare there is another round of betting. This can be tricky if you're one of two players going for one side and there's a lone player going the other way because he or she can just raise the maximum with impunity and you get stuck investing more than you'd like in the hand.

THE ADVANTAGE OF
BEING THE ONLY WOMAN
AT THE TABLE

*Clonie Gowen is one of the best female poker players
in the world. When asked if there were any advantages
to being the only woman at the table, here's what
she said.*

There are so many advantages to being the only
woman. As you move up in level, the advantages don't
jump out at you as much. But they definitely exist at
the lower levels. For one thing, I think that we're more
patient. Men are naturally more competitive and
aggressive; women can still be aggressive, but we're
less likely to let our egos get in the way.

There are several different types of men that will be
sitting down next to you at the poker table that you
have an advantage over. There's the type of guy that's
going to want to flirt with you and get your phone
number. Some of them want to impress you by
beating you but they usually aren't overly aggressive

towards you. They're going to try and play in a lot of pots with you just to try and get some interaction with you. You can tell who they are. If they're constantly trying to chat with you then they're definitely not paying attention to the game. If they're making comments about what you're wearing or telling you that your nails are nice, just look up and smile and play to their personalities. They're going to beat themselves just by playing in too many hands.

Then you have the guy who's coming to play poker because this is his one night out. The last thing he wants to see is another woman because he's trying to get away from his wife and kids. So this guy's going to pay you off more. He's going to be very aggressive towards you, so when you have good hands you're going to make more money with him.

> You just don't hear a man say, "Hey good friend, I have the nuts."

And then there's The Protector. He feels like it's his job to protect you and he'll tell you "Sweetie, I've got the nuts right now," and you'll know just from his tone of voice and how his personality is that he's not lying to you. Now you need to be able to tell that he's telling the truth by watching the patterns through the course of the game. You can't just believe him right off the bat. But he'll tell you honestly what kind of hand he has. You don't see this kind of behavior when men play against other men. You just don't hear a man say, "Hey good friend, I have the nuts." He's just going to play hard against another man, but you will hear a man say that to a woman.

BEST LAS VEGAS POKER ROOMS

Many of the poker choices worldwide are fine – if you can't make it to Las Vegas, Nevada. When it comes to serious poker, however, many purists will nod politely at Aruba, London or even Atlantic City, and head straight for the tables in Vegas. The hierarchy of Vegas poker rooms traces a similar path to the growth of the city and the Strip, with traditional hangouts being eclipsed by glitzy, new locales. Whatever your poker pleasure, chances are Las Vegas has the right game in the right environment for you.

✳ BELLAGIO ✳

Considered by many to be the classiest poker room in the world, the reputation of Bellagio's level of play differs among players. Top pros such as Doyle Brunson and Phil Ivey can frequently be seen playing here. But despite the hotel's lofty nightly rates, all players are welcome, and the results can be a mixed bag. The game's worldwide boom means you're liable to see plenty of card sharks here – and also plenty of fish.

✳ THE PALMS ✳

Yes, really. Thought of by some as more of a hangout for cooler-than-thou 20-somethings than a serious poker destination, The Palms includes several excellent games on its ten tables. If you like to mix glamour with your poker, you stand a good chance of going heads-up against a celebrity on any given night, especially at higher-limit tables. The atmosphere at the tables reflects the atmosphere of the casino itself: wild, loose and never dull.

❇ MIRAGE ❇

When Steve Wynn opened the luxurious Mirage, it was for many years considered *the* place to play casino games on the Strip, including poker. The Bellagio and others have since eclipsed the Mirage's reputation for luxury, but the Mirage's poker room remains legendary. This was long considered the place any serious aspiring pro needed to play to learn the game and the place every frivolous tourist needed to avoid to keep from going broke. More players now means a wider variety of players, but the Mirage remains a prime destination for the best rounders and railbirds alike.

❇ BINION'S HORSESHOE ❇

Benny Binion's pride and joy remained the mecca of the poker world for decades, gaining in popularity as the World Series of Poker debuted in 1970. Hard times would eventually follow, as the senior Binion's passing gave rise to a power struggle among his kids, mismanagement and even a brief closure due to tax problems. Harrah's stepped in to buy it in 2004, though arguably more for the rights to the WSOP than for the casino itself. Still a must on any rounder's play list, the Horseshoe now shares the World Series with the Harrah's-owned Rio. By 2006 the sprawling Rio will host the entire event.

MIKE CARO'S LAWS OF TELLS

Mike Caro, aka "the mad Genius of Poker," is the poker world's foremost authority on tells – the little giveaways that allow you to read your opponents. *Caro's Book of Poker Tells* is one of the most revered and important books about the game ever written. The book goes in-depth in its description of over 50 ways that players commonly reveal the quality of their cards. One key idea is that players who act weak are generally doing so because their hands are strong, and players who act strong are generally doing so because they're bluffing. But there's obviously a lot more to it than that and the book is a must-read for any player looking to get serious about his/her game. Here are ten of Caro's Laws of Tells:

CARO'S LAW OF TELLS #1: Players often stack chips in a manner directly indicative of their style of play. Conservative means conservative; sloppy means sloppy.

CARO'S LAW OF TELLS #4: A trembling bet is a force to be feared.

CARO'S LAW OF TELLS #5: In the absence of any indications to the contrary, call any bettor whose hand covers his mouth.

CARO'S LAW OF TELLS #7: The friendlier a bettor is, the more apt he is to be bluffing.

CARO'S LAW OF TELLS #8: A player secretly glances at his chips only when he's considering a bet – and almost always because he's helped his hand.

CARO'S LAW OF TELLS #11: Disappoint any player who, by acting weak, is seeking your call.

CARO'S LAW OF TELLS #13: Players staring at you are usually less of a threat than players staring away.

CARO'S LAW OF TELLS #14: Players staring at their cards are usually weak.

CARO'S LAW OF TELLS #19: A forceful or exaggerated bet usually means weakness.

CARO'S LAW OF TELLS #24: Beware of sighs and sounds of sorrow.

THE STAR TREK DECK

King of Spades . . . . Captain Kirk

Ace of Diamonds . . . . Romulan Bird of Prey

Queen of Hearts . . . . Orion Slave Woman

Jack of Clubs . . . . Klingon Captain Koloth

Joker . . . . A tribble

STOPS ON THE WORLD POKER TOUR

The lineup gets tweaked a bit each year but this is the one for 2005.

GRAND PRIX DE PARIS
l'Aviation Club de France
in Paris, France

MIRAGE POKER SHOWDOWN
Mirage in Las Vegas, Nevada

LEGENDS OF POKER
Bicycle Casino in
Bell Gardens, California

BORGATA POKER OPEN
Borgata in Atlantic City,
New Jersey

ARUBA POKER CLASSIC
Ultimate Bet Casino in Aruba

**DOYLE BRUNSON NORTH
AMERICA POKER CHAMPIONSHIP**
Bellagio in Las Vegas, Nevada

WORLD POKER FINALS
Foxwoods Resort Casino in
Mashantucket, Connecticut

**FIVE DIAMOND WORLD
POKER CLASSIC**
Bellagio in Las Vegas, Nevada

**POKERSTARS CARIBBEAN
POKER ADVENTURE**
Atlantis Resort in Paradise Island,
Bahamas

WORLD POKER OPEN
Horseshoe Casino and
Gold Strike Casino in Tunica,
Mississippi

L.A. POKER CLASSIC
Commerce in Commerce,
California

**BAY 101 SHOOTING
STARS OF POKER**
Bay 101 in San Jose, California

PARTY POKER MILLION
Party Poker's Cruise to Mexico

WORLD POKER CHALLENGE
Reno Hilton in Reno, Nevada

WPT WORLD CHAMPIONSHIP
Bellagio in Las Vegas, Nevada

POKER FASHION

Though once in a blue moon you'll see someone in old-West type finery in a cardroom, the days of suits and ties, Crandall Addington style, are over. Now you're more likely to see a pro dressed in casual clothes, with sunglasses and a baseball cap thrown in for good measure. Whatever you choose to wear, make sure it's something that you're comfortable in.

> Be wary of overdressing the part.

If you feel like poker is your job and you're comfortable and confident in business attire, wear that designer suit. Maybe the table image you're going for will be complemented by dressing like a tourist, so bust out the Hawaiian shirt or the polyester one with the card suits on fire emblazoned on the back. As for wearing poker-specific merchandise, once again, that's a personal decision. One person might want to show off that pleather jacket they won on their favorite online site. Someone else might hold to the ideal that you never wear the Springsteen shirt to the Springsteen concert.

Be wary of overdressing the part. This quote comes straight out of Phil Gordon and Jonathan Grotenstein's *Poker: The Real Deal:*

"Wearing sunglasses at the final table of the World Series can give you the look and edge of a champion. Those same sunglasses at a $2/$4 table will probably make you look like a jackass."

Traditionally in home poker, each player tosses a certain amount in the pot, called an ante. Ante is just a term that means "to come before." They assure that the players are playing for *something*.

Without them, there'd rarely be a reason to play any but the very best hands and poker would involve a lot more sitting around and shuffling. Say there are six of you. The typical way it works is that each of you tosses in a dollar for a starting pot of $6. But there's a better way to do this. Rather than suffer through an evening where on every other hand you and your fellow players are trying to figure out who forgot to ante, why not have the dealer ante the whole $6 for the whole table on his or her deal? The amount of time you'll get to spend actually playing poker will skyrocket.

> Ante is just a term that means "to come before."

The only additional, extremely minor complication is that you need to make sure that everyone in the game deals the same number of times through the course of the evening. If this task is too daunting, stick to Uno.

♥ ♦ ♠

THE RULES OF FIVE-CARD STUD

Another one of the oldest poker variations, Five-Card Stud is the game they play in *The Cincinnati Kid*. Each player antes. The dealer deals a hole card down and a door card up to each player, followed by a round of betting, which is started by the high card. If there are two up cards of the same suit, the betting is opened by the high card to the dealer's left, as in Seven-Card Stud. The first round of betting is followed by another up card, and another round of betting. This is repeated twice more, followed by a showdown.

ROUNDS

It's not a bad idea in your home game to play in rounds. Even if you're doing dealer's choice, you have every player deal out the game that the first dealer calls. Then the player to the first dealer's left calls out a new game and that is played around. The process continues around the table. The advantage of playing in rounds is that it's easier to create a flow when you're playing the same game six times in a row than when you're changing gears constantly. It also takes away any positional advantages that the dealer might have, depending on the game.

WHAT GAME SHOULD WE PLAY?

With home poker, there are a lot of different ways to go. These days, home poker No-Limit Hold'em tournaments are all the rage and there are some good reasons why. That notwithstanding, old-fashioned dealer's choice still has a place in the world. Just like it sounds, with dealer's choice the rotating dealer is allowed to call any game he or she chooses that fits within the house rules (some home games don't allow wild card games, for example).

MAKING THE TRANSITION
FROM ONLINE TO THE CASINO

 Scott Fischman is one of bigtime poker's youngest and most exciting competitors. A former dealer and a member of the poker collective known as The Crew, Scott turned the poker world on its head by winning back-to-back gold bracelets at the 2004 World Series of Poker. Here are his thoughts about the biggest differences between playing online and the cardroom.

The biggest differences between playing online and playing in person are the speed of the game and the fact that you're sitting in front of actual people. The major thing to consider is that when you're used to playing online, play in the cardroom is going to be a lot slower and a little bit more boring. So you're really going to have to do your best to stay focused with the change in atmosphere. The other thing that's really important is the concept of table image. Now that everybody can see you and you can see them, it's a little different than playing online. Online, you really just play your cards and you can't really get a read off people, nor can they get a read off you. When you get to the casino, you have to be aware of how you look, how you dress, how other people perceive you. And you also have to pay attention to those things when it comes to your opponents. Those are the biggest differences.

TABLE IMAGE

Table image is important for a lot of reasons. How you choose to handle your table image really depends on the type of game you play. You can create your own character, so to speak. Depending on what your style of play is, you need to be aware of how you want other people to see you. Maybe you're a tight player and you want to be seen as a tight player. Maybe you're a crazy maniac and you want to be seen that way. There are different ways to play with table image.

Your table image sets the tone of the game and it's one of the biggest reasons why an opponent is going to play a hand against you in a certain way. If you can determine how they're going to play hands against you based on how they view you, then you can counteract how they're playing against you and manipulate the situation to your advantage. You have to know how they view you so you know how they're going to play against you. Do they think you're a loose player so they're going to call you more? Do they think you're a tight player and they're going to respect your raises? There's a lot of ways to play with it.

SCOTT FISCHMAN ON HIS OWN TABLE IMAGE

When I first started, there weren't as many young players. I was 22 or 23 years old and probably looked even younger than that, and I was underestimated and I wasn't known and I used that to my advantage. My table image was an empty seat. That's why my online handle is EmptySeat88. Players just looked right through me. They didn't think I had any ability, they thought I was just a kid. I had all the experience of playing online. I felt like I was an experienced player but I didn't look that way. That allowed me to take advantage of other players and be successful. A lot of the younger players today don't have that same advantage.

SCOTT FISCHMAN ON THE SOCIAL PRESSURE OF THE CARDROOM

When you're playing in person, there's social pressure. Online, there's none. You can curse at somebody, you can bluff as much as you want, and when your cards flip over and you have nothing and you've lost $1,000, no one looks you in the eye and says, "My God, you're an idiot." But when you're playing live, there's a lot of natural, social pressure that makes you not want to look like a total idiot and make a fool of yourself.

But you don't want to yield to that pressure. You want to play your same game. You've learned to play online and that's your style and if it works and you're successful you can't let those things change your game when you sit down. You have to try and visualize an environment and make yourself comfortable.

VISUALIZING YOUR ENVIRONMENT

In a way, you have to trick yourself. When I first started, I would change things around in my mind to make them the same as what I was used to. One thing I used to do was to change the limits in my mind. Let's say I was playing in a tournament and we started with $10,000 in chips like they do in a lot of the big tournaments. Well, online we'd only usually start with maybe $1,000 in chips. So I would divide everything by ten and try and trick myself that I was still playing online in that tournament where I'm very accustomed to the limits and the chips and the structure. Once you start thinking about the money, you're in trouble.

MATCH THE PLAYER WITH
THE FASHION ACCESSORY

1. PHIL LAAK

2. AMARILLO SLIM

3. DANIEL NEGREANU

4. GREG RAYMER

5. PHIL IVEY

6. ANY MEMBER OF THE HENDON MOB

BLUFFING ESSENTIALS

Matt Lessinger is a poker pro and the author of The
Book of Bluffs *(Warner Books, 2005), which does for
bluffing what Mike Caro did for tells. He boils bluffing
down to the three Cs: creativity, confidence and
cojones, and his book tells you how to develop all three.
Here are some of his key rules for bluffing.*

1. Betting when last to act – even when you have bad
   cards – is one of the simplest forms of bluffing, yet
   probably the most vital to long-term success. If the
   people betting before you look like they have nothing, this is the time to try and steal the pot.

2. Even if you're not last to act, looking at the players
   on your left before acting is absolutely indispensa-
   ble; you can't be a successful bluffer without finding
   a way of getting extra information about what your
   opponents are likely to do. When you see that weakness, attack it. Conversely, if you don't have any reason to think the player or players on your left will
   fold, especially at the end of the hand, then your
   bluff is unlikely to work.

3. Learn to look for clues that other players in your game
   are on a draw. If you're isolated against one opponent
   and he's on a draw, that opponent might be a good
   candidate to bluff. And when it looks like they've
   missed their draw, go for the kill and attack them.

4. When you're attempting a bluff, make sure to properly sell your hand. From the start, ask yourself,

"How would I play if I had the hand I'm representing?" and stick to that. If you can convince your opponent that you have a made hand from the get go, you'll cause him to lose confidence and set him up to fold to you even if he has the better hand. Similarly, if you've represented a weak hand from the start, it's going to be very difficult to successfully bluff at the end of the hand.

5. Know your opponents. If they're not paying attention then you're not going to be able to bluff them. If you're playing in a game where most players are there just for the action and they call a lot, don't mess around with bluffing. Their own loose play is going to beat them anyway, so wait until you have premium cards and then take their money.

6. If a player is showing his hand to another player during play, watch closely – it's very likely that one of them will betray what he's holding, enabling you to bet and win when you normally would have folded. Likewise, you might also pick up that they have strong cards and save a bet that way.

7. You never want to get caught bluffing. But you don't want to fear getting caught either. If you're found out, you'll set it up that you'll get called later on when you really do have the best hand. Of course, bluffing again later might be tricky.

8. A good bluff tells a story your opponent will understand. When you're bluffing, don't send off contradictory signals that will confuse your opponent because confusion leads to being called. Follow a believable pattern and let them fold in a way that will let them sleep at night, thinking it was a good fold, not a place they should have called.

SOME THOUGHTS ON RABBIT HUNTING

Rabbit hunting – the act of looking at the cards once
the hand is over to see what would have happened if
you hadn't folded – is common practice in a lot of
home games and even in some cardrooms. However,
it's not something that's a good idea if you want to
develop a winning mindset for poker. Winning at poker
– or any form of gambling – should be all about making good decisions, not getting favorable outcomes. If
someone offers you $2 if a coin comes up heads and
you have to pay them only $1 if it comes up tails,
you've got to take that bet. It doesn't matter if you get
a terrible outcome, like the coin coming up tails eight
times in a row. You'll have made a good decision. So it
is in poker. If you fold because the odds weren't right
to call, then it shouldn't matter if your miracle card
would have come on the river, you made the right
decision by walking away. Players who get lucky and
suckout will eventually be giving their money back to
you anyway. So skip the rabbit hunting. It's not the
specifics of the outcomes of the cards that matter but
the process of the decisions behind them.

FAMOUS POKER DEATHS

There's a story in Andy Bellin's book, *Poker Nation*, about a famous American Indian poker player from the old west known as Poker Tom. Tom cheated a merchant named Ah Tia out of $2,000. Two days after, Tom's remains were supposedly fed to members of his own tribe in a stew that Ah Tia made for a country fair.

James Butler Hickok, known as Wild Bill, was a professional gambler and legendary gunslinger. In 1876, during a poker game at Nuttal and Mann's Saloon No. 10 in Deadwood, South Dakota, he was shot in the back and killed by Jack McCall. If you don't already know what hand he was holding, see page 115.

Jack "Treetop" Straus was a beloved member of the poker community. He won the 1982 World Series of Poker and was one of the best Hold'em players of his day. In 1988, he suffered a heart attack and died at the poker table in a high-stakes game in Los Angeles, supposedly in the midst of one final bluff.

ODDS AGAINST GETTING DEALT VARIOUS FIVE-CARD POKER HANDS

ROYAL STRAIGHT FLUSH	649,739-1	STRAIGHT	254-1
STRAIGHT FLUSH	64,973-1	THREE OF A KIND	46-1
FOUR OF A KIND	4,164-1	TWO PAIR	20-1
FULL HOUSE	693-1	ONE PAIR	1.25-1
FLUSH	508-1	NO PAIR	EVEN

MATT MATROS ON MATH

Matt Matros is a professional poker player and poker writer. He's the author of a really smart book called The Making of a Poker Player, *which combines his narrative of making it as a poker pro with poker instruction. Matros finished third in the World Poker Tour Championship in 2004. A numbers expert, he graduated from Yale with a B.S. in math with distinction in the major in 1999. Here are his thoughts on some of the most important math concepts to the average poker player.*

EXPECTED VALUE

The long run profit or loss of a given play is called the expected value (EV). In poker, EV is everything. EV is God. If you make a positive EV play, then it doesn't matter if you win or lose on a particular hand, you've still made money overall. This concept can be extended to every stage of the hand. The question "Should I call preflop?" is equivalent to asking "Does calling with this hand have positive EV in this situation?" How the cards fall is beyond our control. The only thing we can do as players is put our chips in with positive EV ("getting the best of it," as players like to say). Do that often enough and the cards will take care of themselves.

POT ODDS

Pot odds measure the amount of money in the pot at any one time against the amount of money you'd have to put in the pot to call. This really comes into play when you think you're behind in a hand but you have a draw, or on the river when you're going to get to see the other person's hand if you call. If there's $50 in the pot and it's going to cost you $10 to call and you have a better than one-in-six chance of winning the hand, then that's a good call. Conversely, if there is $50 in the pot and you have worse than a one in six chance of winning the pot, it's a bad call. Your potential payoffs must exceed the chances of your having the best hand if you want to win in the long run.

GAME THEORY

Game theory is a branch of mathematics that deals with decision making. It's often used in economics and business to determine the right strategies to use in different situations. Game theory has poker applications as well. If you were to use a game theory optimal strategy at the poker table, you could tell anyone exactly what your strategy was and you'd be able to win in the long run anyway, assuming you had no obvious tells. If I'm re-raising all-in on the flop and my opponent asks me if I want him to call, I'm going to say "Do what you want." Sometimes I'll have a huge hand, sometimes I'll be on a draw, but either way I'm going to be a winner in the long run. This is because I'm raising with the correct proportion of draws and made hands so that my EV is the same no matter what my opponent does.

MORE MATT MATROS ON MATH
RULE OF FOUR

 A quick way to figure out your chances of making your hand after the flop in Hold'em is to figure out the amount of possible outs you have and multiply that by four. Say you have four to a flush. That means there are nine cards that could possibly help you. You have two chances to catch them, one on the turn and one on the river. Simply multiply nine by four and you get 36 – meaning you have an approximately 36% chance of making your hand. That percentage translates to odds of roughly 2-1 against you making your flush. So it'd be a good idea to call if the pot is paying off 2-1 or better for every $1 you have to bet.

> It's not perfect but it's close enough for most situations you'll find yourself in.

If you're in the same situation on the turn, you have one less chance to make your hand, so instead of multiplying your number of outs by four, you multiply by two. For the example above, you'd multiply 9 by 2 for an 18% chance of making the flush. So the pot would need to be paying off 4-1 or better for you to call.

The more outs you have, the less accurate this type of rough calculation becomes (and the less it matters, because with very many outs you almost always want to play your hand aggressively). It's not perfect but it's close enough for most situations you'll find yourself in.

MATT MATROS ON READING
YOUR OPPONENT

Making reads requires poker skills that are separate from math, but in the end you need to be able to convert those reads to a percentage. You need to be able to say that there's a 90% chance he has this kind of hand, a 10% chance he has another kind of hand. You need to ask yourself, "How big is my hand? How big is my opponent's hand? What chance do I have to win?" That's a good habit to get into – you can even work on it when you're away from the table by asking yourself questions like, "When I read that guy for a big pair, what did that mean in terms of percentages, and what exact range of hands did I give him?"

MATT MATROS ON THE IMPORTANCE OF
LUCK IN TOURNAMENT PLAY

Luck is an important factor on any given day but not in the long run. The poker players out there who think they're going to win every tournament they play aren't going to do very well. If you can get your chips in when you're a 55% favorite, that's great. Investing in those kind of spots is how tournaments are won. And sure, amateurs are going to win tournaments. But you can't worry about that. Your job is not to avoid taking risks – it's to put yourself in the best position to get lucky by making sure you're getting the best of it. Once you accept that, you're in a much better position to be a successful tournament player.

THE ORIGINS OF POKER

There are nearly as many theories about how the game of poker developed as there are variations of the game itself. While that's a slight exaggeration, it is agreed upon that, like baseball, poker evolved over time from a number of different games brought to America by various immigrant cultures.

One of the most important forbearers to modern poker is a Persian card game from the 17th century called As-Naz. That game was played by Persian settlers in New Orleans circa the late 1820s. The people living there at the time were largely French and were familiar with a game that originated in France in the 18th century called Poque (perhaps mispronounced po-kuh by the locals). To complicate matters further, some say the game began incorporating aspects of a German game called Pochspiel, which contained bluffing (though some sources claim that bluffing was already an element of Poque). The combination of "Poque" and/or "Pochspiel" with "As-Naz" became "Pokas." Ultimately, Pokas changed over time to the term poker we still use today.

♥ ♣ ♦ ♠

MORE ON POKER ORIGINS

No matter what your heritage, there's a good chance you can claim that your ancestors are the true fathers of poker!

ANY MUSLIM COUNTRY: The first decks of cards with four suits (cups and swords, added to the Chinese circles and bamboos) came from the Islamic world. The concept of "court cards" came from there as well.

CHINA: Around 950 A.D., a Chinese emperor introduced a game called "domino cards" or "paper dominoes," which influenced later card games that evolved into poker.

DENMARK: The Danish word for "devil" is "pokker." Coincidence? You decide.

EGYPT: As far back as the 12th or 13th century, the Egyptians played card games. Their resemblance to modern poker is unknown but it's certainly possible that they contained similar aspects.

ENGLAND: A number of early card games, including Primero, Faro and Brag became very popular in England in the 16th century. The English introduced the concept of casino-style card play, where an indeterminate number of players would play against a single banker ("or dealer").

FRANCE: Poque was a game that had the specific suits for the cards still used today and had elements of bluffing and betting.

GERMANY: Pochspiel may have its roots in Poque, but many claim that it was actually the Germans who introduced bluffing into the game.

INDIA: The Persian game, As-Naz, originally derived from a game called Ganjifa, so in a way, Ganjifa is the great-grandfather of the modern game.

ITALY: Primero was a Renaissance card game with some similarities to poker whose play was described in writing by an Italian mathematician in the 16th century.

PERSIA: As-Naz, a card game with suits, hierarchical card rankings and betting rounds, is generally accepted as the father of modern poker.

CHEATING AND POKER

From its earliest days, poker has always been a game that attracted cheaters. At least it's attracted professional sharps whose goal was to lure in a sucker and separate him from his money. There are two theories about the etymology of the word poker that incorporate the very idea that the game is, shall we say, not always on the up and up.

POKE: An underworld term used by pickpockets. One story has it that an "r" was added to the end so that a cardsharp's victims wouldn't realize that they were being hustled.

HOCUS POCUS: Then, as now, hocus pocus was a term used by magicians to describe their "magic." Some think that poker comes from this phrase, again implying that a newcomer to a game of sharps didn't exactly have a fair shot.

TEGWAR

In the movie *Bang the Drum Slowly*, the ballplayers play a game called TEGWAR, which may harken back to the early days of riverboat poker, where the "professional" players would find a patsy on board and separate him from his money (not always by the most honest of means). The idea of TEGWAR was that the players would find an unsuspecting teammate or a fan in the lobby looking to spend time with them and play this new card game. The thing was, while the sucker might start off on a hot streak, in the end the players always won. The players weren't exactly cheating, it's just that the rules of TEGWAR changed as the game went along, according to the players' whims. TEGWAR — The Exciting Game Without Any Rules.

HOW TO SHUFFLE

When learning to shuffle, there's no need to rush. Go slowly and concentrate on each step. Also note that new cards can be a little inflexible and therefore difficult to shuffle. You can bend them to loosen them up but be very careful not to leave any marks on the cards or they'll be useless.

1. Divide the deck into two approximately even stacks.

2. Placing one stack in either hand, put your thumb under the cards and your forefinger, middle finger and ring finger on the top.

3. Hold your hands close and at a slight angle. Your thumbs should be within an inch of each other *(fig. 1)*.

4. Raise up the inside part of each stack of cards with your thumb while pushing down on the outside part of each stack with your fingers *(fig. 2)*.

5. Now, the tricky part. Slowly move your thumbs out from under the stacks, releasing one card at a time, first from one stack, then the other *(fig. 3)*. Combine the two stacks entirely in this way. (You might want to practice this one hand at a time.)

6. Push the shuffled cards back into one pile. Repeat.

| **fig. 1** | **fig. 2** | **fig. 3** |

THE TOP FIVE BLUFFS IN
WORLD SERIES OF POKER HISTORY

1. 2003 / CHRIS MONEYMAKER: It was down to just Moneymaker and Sammy Farha at the final table and the board showed 9 ♠ -2 ♦ -6 ♠ -8 ♠ . Farha held Q ♠ -9 ♥ , giving him top pair and a flush draw. He bet $300,000. Moneymaker raised him $500,000; Farha called. The river card was the 3 ♥ . Farha checked and Moneymaker went all-in. After some deliberation, Farha folded. Less than an hour later, Moneymaker went on to make poker history by winning the World Series. What cards did Moneymaker have in that hand to play so boldly? Nothing. Just K ♠ -7 ♥ for king high.

2. 1988 / JOHNNY CHAN: A reverse bluff really, made all the more famous by *Rounders*. Chan and Erik Seidel were heads up at the final table. After the flop, Chan had the nut straight. He held J-9 and the board was Q-10-8. Seidel held Q-7, giving him top pair. Both players checked after the flop and on the turn. The river card was a rag and Seidel moved all-in, thinking his queens were best. Chan instantly called, knowing Seidel had fallen into his trap and that he was going to win the World Series of Poker for the second year in a row.

3. 1997 / STU UNGAR: With four players left at the final table, Ungar had the lead but Ron Stanley was beginning to catch up. The other players folded before the flop. It came A ♠ 9 ♥ 6 ♠ . Both players checked, something Ungar had done previously when paired an ace on the flop. An 8 came on the turn; Stanley bet $25,000 (he held 9-7 for a pair of nines and an open-ended straight draw). Ungar raised $60,000 and

Stanley called. The river card was a king. Stanley checked, Ungar bet $225,000, and Stanley folded. Then Ungar revealed that he was holding a worthless Q-10. Stanley exited the tournament shortly thereafter and Ungar went on to win his third and final World Series title.

4. 1978 / BOBBY BALDWIN: Baldwin and Crandall Addington were heads up at the final table with Addington in the lead. Addington raised before the flop and Baldwin called, holding the 9♥ and 10♥. The flop came Q-4-3 with two diamonds and Baldwin bet. Addington called immediately, surely suggesting that he had a hand better than Baldwin's. The next card was the A♦ and Baldwin moved all-in. Addington folded, even though he still had the best hand (we don't know exactly what hand because there was no hole-cam back then). Baldwin never looked back and went on to win the tournament.

5. 1984 / COWBOY WOLFORD: It was down to three players at the final table, Byron "Cowboy" Wolford, Jesse Alto and Jack Keller. Wolford held nothing, but when the flop came A♠, 9♠, K♦, Wolford bet $15,000, which Alto called. After the K♥ came on the turn, Wolford bet $40,000, which Alto also called. The river card was the 2♠ and Cowboy went all-in, pushing his last $101,000 in the pot. After a couple of minutes of intense deliberation, Alto put his cards face down. Then the Cowboy revealed his stone bluff, showing his 3-5 offsuit. Alto instantly went on tilt and bluffed away his money to Keller in the next few hands. Keller went on to win the tournament.

THE RULES FOR TEXAS HOLD'EM

Each player gets dealt two cards face down. Then there's a round of betting. The next three cards are community cards, common to all the players' hands, and they are placed face up in the middle of the table. This is called the flop, and after it occurs, there is another round of betting. The fourth card, called fourth street or the turn, is also a community card dealt face up in the middle. Another round of betting follows. The fifth card, occasionally called fifth street but more often called the river, is the final face up community card. The final round of betting comes after the river is dealt. Players must make their best possible five-card hands out of the two in their hand and the five on the board.

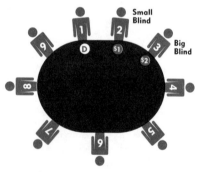

In Texas Hold'em, there isn't a traditional ante. Instead, there are blinds that are designed to stimulate the action in much the same way. The player directly to the dealer's left is in the small blind and typically he or she will post an amount approximately half the size of the lower limit in the game. If you're playing $2-$4 Hold'em, the small blind might be $1.50. The player to the left of the small blind is known as the big blind, and he or she has to post an amount equal to the lower limit. In the case of that same $2-$4 game, $2.

The player to the left of the big blind (#4 in the diagram opposite), who is said to be "under the gun," starts the action on the first round of betting, before the flop. After the first round of betting, the first remaining player to the left of the dealer, whether in the blinds or not, is first to act.

 If you're playing in a cardroom where there's an actual dealer, one of the players at the table still must be the nominal "dealer," and he or she will get a little button indicating this (this player is said to be "on the button"). Because position is such a big advantage in Hold'em, the dealer, whether actual or nominal, rotates to the left after each hand, also moving the blinds one spot to the left.

BURN AND TURN

It's conventional in Hold'em and other flop games for the dealer to discard or "burn" a card before the flop and before the cards on the turn and the river. After the first card is burned by being placed face down in front of the dealer, the next card is turned over for all to see. This keeps the top card safe from being accidentally shown and also theoretically makes it tougher for a mechanic to manipulate the deck.

HIGH-LOW SPLIT, 8 MUST: The pot is split between the high and low hands. You must have an 8-high or lower to take the low. Cards speak.

CRAZY PINEAPPLE: You get three cards to start instead of two, and you must dump one of them after the flop.

LAZY PINEAPPLE: You get three cards, which you can keep until the end of the hand. You're allowed to use up to two of the cards in your hand but not all three.

LAZY PINEAPPLE HIGH-LOW SPLIT: In the high-low version of lazy pineapple you can also use up to two of your hole cards with the board cards to make your best high hand. You can simultaneously use a different combination of up to two of your three hole cards with the board cards to go low. The ace plays high-low and the cards speak.

REVERSE HOLD'EM: In regular Hold'em, of course, you flop three cards, then one, then another. In reverse Hold'em, first one card is placed face up and bet on, then another, and then three get turned over at once.

HUMP HOLD'EM: Same as above but the community cards come one-three-one.

DOUBLE FLOP TEXAS HOLD'EM: Instead of one flop, you get two – one that forms an upper board and one that forms a lower board. Same deal with the turn and the river, one each for the upper and lower boards. At the end of the hand, you must pick which board you want to use and make your best hand between your cards and either the upper or the lower.

THE BEST STARTING HANDS
IN TEXAS HOLD'EM

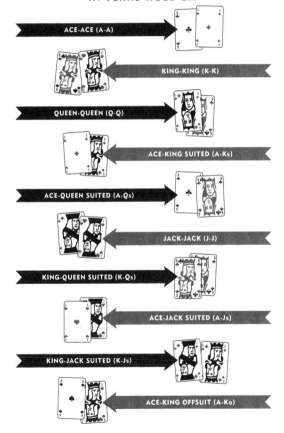

ACE-ACE (A-A)

KING-KING (K-K)

QUEEN-QUEEN (Q-Q)

ACE-KING SUITED (A-Ks)

ACE-QUEEN SUITED (A-Qs)

JACK-JACK (J-J)

KING-QUEEN SUITED (K-Qs)

ACE-JACK SUITED (A-Js)

KING-JACK SUITED (K-Js)

ACE-KING OFFSUIT (A-Ko)

POKER AND ART

So which artist's work is the most recognized in the world? Da Vinci? Picasso? Dali? Maybe. But according to one new survey, published on the always-reliable Internet, the most recognizable painting in the world is by a guy named Cassius Marcellus Coolidge and is called "A Friend In Need." You might know it better as "Dogs Playing Poker," though as Dan Barry quipped in *The New York Times*, that description "is not unlike referring to one of Van Gogh's self-portraits as 'Guy Missing an Ear.'" The painting shows two small dogs cheating at poker (Five-Card Draw) at a table with five larger dogs.

> Calling Coolidge's painting "Dogs Playing Poker" is "not unlike referring to one of Van Gogh's self-portraits as 'Guy Missing an Ear.'"

Coolidge grew up on a farm in western New York before leaving in the 1860s to travel around the United States and Europe. He tried a variety of professions: druggist, banker, cartoonist, newspaper writer, playwright (he even wrote and produced a comic opera) and, of course, painter – of both street signs and canvas. But his specialty was the odd sort of masculine, anthropomorphic art evidenced in "A Friend In Need."

Cigar companies were his first clients, who used his prints as giveaways. He got his big break in the early 1900s when a series of sixteen of his paintings of dogs behaving like people were distributed by the printer Brown & Bigelow. Nine of them were of dogs playing poker. As a side note, Coolidge was obsessed with one particular hand – four aces – which appears in four of

the nine poker paint-
ings. The images were
reprinted in great num-
bers on advertising
posters, calendars and
prints. In more recent
years, the images have
been reproduced in a
wide variety of places,
from black velvet can-
vasses to T-shirts to
poker chips to truly
hideous neckties.

He didn't create any significant art after the early
1900s, but he did marry and have a daughter. Coolidge
died at age 89 in 1934. But his work lives on in dens,
basements, bathrooms, barrooms and pool halls
across America. In 2005, two of his originals sold for
over $500,000.

**THE REAL NAMES OF
CASSIUS COOLIDGE'S DOGS
PLAYING POKER PAINTINGS**

A FRIEND IN NEED
A BOLD BLUFF
HIS STATION AND FOUR ACES
PINCHED WITH FOUR ACES
POKER SYMPATHY
SITTING UP WITH A SICK FRIEND
A STRANGER IN CAMP
POST MORTEM
WATERLOO

RULES FOR OMAHA

Many of the conventions in Omaha are the same as in Hold'em. The biggest difference is that each player starts with four hole cards instead of two. After the cards are dealt, there is a round of betting. This is followed by a flop of three face-up community cards in the middle of the table and another round of betting. Then, as in Hold'em, there are separate rounds of betting for both the turn and the river, followed by a showdown.

The other incredibly important difference between Hold'em and Omaha is that in all forms of Omaha, *you must use two of the four cards from your hand and three from the board.*

The blind structure works just like in Hold'em (see pg. 62).

Omaha is frequently played pot-limit (see pg. 14).

♥ ♣ ♦ ♠

OMAHA HIGH-LOW SPLIT

Even more popular than Pot-Limit Omaha is Omaha High-Low Split. The rules are the same as those described above except the pot is split between the high and low hands. The game is also called Omaha/8 for short because to win the low you need to have an 8-high or lower (see pg. 95). It's played cards speak (see pg. 33) and it's possible to scoop the pot and win both high and low. A great game for action as there are many, many hands that have the potential to lead to something.

SOME GREAT STARTING
HANDS IN OMAHA HIGH

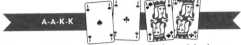

A·A·K·K

(or any pair of aces and kings, but it's best if the kings
are suited to the aces – this goes for all these hands)

A·A·10·J

A·A·Q·Q

(really two aces with any pair, the higher the better,
especially if the high cards are suited to the aces)

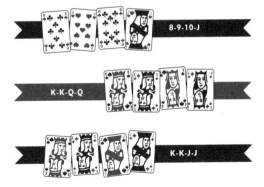

8·9·10·J

K·K·Q·Q

K·K·J·J

ROBERT WILLIAMSON III'S KEY TO SUCCESS IN OMAHA HIGH-LOW, EIGHT OR BETTER (AKA OMAHA/8)

Robert Williamson III, recently called "The Joker of Poker" by ABC's Primetime Live, *is a top professional in both tournaments and cash games, known for his particular prowess at Pot Limit Omaha (to get his advice on that game, however, you'll have to buy his book, if he ever gets around to writing it). He has also done poker analysis for GSN's* Poker Royale *and UPN's* Ultimate Poker Challenge. *Here he offers his key to success at Omaha/8.*

In Omaha/8, you have to play two-way hands. That's why an ace is so powerful because you want to play hands that have value towards high and low. If you just have low hands – hands that lend towards low or that need to draw for low – you're just playing for half the pot. You want to play hands that have two ways to win, flush draw, straight draw or a pair and a low draw. You have to have some sort of high to justify getting involved with a low draw and a lot of beginners think that drawing at that A-2 the whole way is a good play and it's not. If you get into a two- or three-way pot, you're playing for maybe a quarter of the pot or just half the pot at the most. You're not giving yourself a chance to play for the whole pot. If you already have a lot of money committed to the pot – if three people raised pre flop – that's different. There, you're playing for a lot of equity. But if you have one bet before the flop and you've got a cold call A-2 drawing for a little bit of the pot, it's not profitable.

One other aspect about Omaha/8 that's not that commonly known is that if you're in a multiway pot – if you're playing against lots of opponents – and you have a high-only hand, there's a premium on your hand. Normally speaking, when there's multiway action, that means that a lot of the little cards are dead. That means that there are a lot of big cards that are still left in the deck to come.

♥ ♦ ♣ ♠

ROBERT WILLIAMSON III ON A COMMON MISTAKE IN TOURNAMENT PLAY

When you're developing your tournament game plan, you need to be ready to change it the moment you get your table assignment. Each table assignment should change your strategy for the whole tournament. In other words, if you've got a table that's extremely tight and you know the structure of the tournament is fast and you're going to have to play fast, you might not want to play fast after all because you know the rest of the table is going to play tight. You might have a table that fits the tournament but it doesn't fit the style of the table you drew. I see that mistake from pros more than I see it from amateurs. Feeling the pace of the table the first 30 minutes or an hour you're playing is very important.

THE FALSE DOVETAIL SHUFFLE

This cheater's shuffle can be used to place cards throughout the deck. Not recommended unless you have no fear of ending up at the bottom of the Gowanus Canal in cement shoes.

1. Divide the deck in half as you would for an honest shuffle.

2. To keep the top card where it is, just shuffle normally and make sure that the top card is the last one to fall. To place several cards at the top of the deck, make sure that the top half is cut fatter than the lower half. The bottom will be properly shuffled before your placed cards fall on top.

If you do both these things at once, you'll know the identity of cards on the top and the bottom of the deck.

3. To place the bottom card or cards, make sure they fall first, then complete the shuffle as normal. If you do both of these things at once, you'll know the identity of cards on the top and the bottom of the deck.

4. Once you've mastered those techniques, it's time to get on to the more serious business of doing a completely fake shuffle. This time, you want the upper half of the deck cut thinner than the lower half.

5. Shuffle as you would normally, but make sure that it's just the outside corners of the cards that touch.

Make sure you finish with a card from the thinner part of the deck on top.

6. Next, bring your fingers together the way you would if you were finishing a legit shuffle. But, and this is very important, press down slightly with your hand that holds the fatter part of the deck. The corners should come undone. The trick is to accomplish this while moving your hands together as if finishing the shuffle as normal. Then just slide the fat half on top of the thin half. You're going to need to practice this last part a lot to make it look natural. The faster you make the move, the better.

7. Good luck! And don't blame the publisher if you get your thumbs broken.

POKER IN THE LOUNGE
Looking for that extra edge? Get your guests drunk!

1.5 oz of tequila
.5 oz of triple sec
4 oz of pineapple juice

Pour all ingredients into shaker. Fill a highball glass almost full of ice cubes and dump ice into shaker. Shake well and pour drink into highball glass. Garnish with a lime wedge and serve.

SCOTT FISCHMAN ON TOURNAMENT PLAY

Stack control and stack play are a big part of becoming a better player. You can learn a lot about how to play in all those different situations by playing tournaments online. Over time, you'll get to be a lot better.

It's tough to give specific advice about what to do when in tournaments because it really depends on a lot of variables. If I have a big stack early, I might play really tight because there's nothing to gain by loosening up – you can only hurt yourself. But if I have a big stack late, I'm definitely going to loosen up because other people at the table are going to be tightening up, trying to get into the money or work their way up. So a big stack doesn't always mean play tight; small stack doesn't always mean play loose. It all depends on where you're at and those are things that you'll learn over time.

THE TIME TO GET AGGRESSIVE

You need to think about changing your strategy any time that the blinds and antes are equal to 20% of your stack. (Editor's note: As many tournaments progress, all players at the table have to post an ante when they're not in the blinds.) In other words, if you could only go five full rounds until you're out, that's the point where you really need to open up and get aggressive, maybe even a little reckless. Sometimes in that situation you have to play without even looking at your cards. If you're on the button or the cutoff (the seat to the left of the button) and your stack is down to 20% of the blinds and antes, you push all-in. Because you're going to be out soon anyway if you just sit there waiting for cards so you might as well at least give yourself some chance to stay in. It really all depends on what your stack is in relation to the structure of the tournament.

♥ ♣ ♦ ♠

SCOTT FISCHMAN ON SELF-CONTROL

Sometimes I struggle with myself. I already know how to play all my cards in every situation but sometimes my own lack of control will get me into trouble in a tournament. One of the biggest keys to being successful is knowing yourself and being able to control yourself. It's something you can learn somewhat but it's also something you're born with, at least partially. It comes up in every tournament. It's a question of being able to execute the correct play every time, no matter how you're feeling. A situation will come up and you know what the right play is and you have to control yourself every time to do the right thing. It's very hard to do that. It could be boredom; maybe you want to do something other than the norm. It could be you're on tilt because you're on a downswing. Or maybe you've been winning and you're overconfident because of that. But you can't let those things affect you – you have to make the right decision every time.

> It's a question of being able to execute the correct play every time, no matter how you're feeling.

Online it's even easier to lose control. You're alone, it's faster, you don't have that social pressure. You need that patience and discipline wherever you're playing or you're never going to be a winner.

TEN GREAT STARTING HANDS IN OMAHA/8

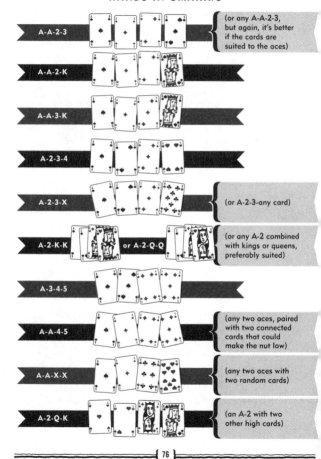

A-A-2-3 (or any A-A-2-3, but again, it's better if the cards are suited to the aces)

A-A-2-K

A-A-3-K

A-2-3-4

A-2-3-X (or A-2-3-any card)

A-2-K-K or A-2-Q-Q (or any A-2 combined with kings or queens, preferably suited)

A-3-4-5

A-A-4-5 (any two aces, paired with two connected cards that could make the nut low)

A-A-X-X (any two aces with two random cards)

A-2-Q-K (an A-2 with two other high cards)

FOUR ARTISTS WHO SANG DIFFERENT SONGS CALLED "THE GAMBLER"

Kenny Rogers

Woody Guthrie

Leonard Cohen

Emerson, Lake and Palmer

♥ ♣ ♦ ♠

ONE WOMAN WHO SANG A SONG CALLED "GAMBLER"

Madonna

♥ ♣ ♦ ♠

TWO ARTISTS WHO SANG A SONG CALLED "FIVE-CARD STUD"

Buckwheat Zydeco

Ace Frehley

♥ ♣ ♦ ♠

A FEW OTHER SONGS THAT MENTION POKER:

"Tango Till They're Sore" by Tom Waits

"Lily, Rosemary and the Jack of Hearts" by Bob Dylan

"Riverboat Gambler" by Carly Simon

"Little Queen of Spades" by Robert Johnson

"Turn of a Friendly Card" by Alan Parsons

"Poker" by Electric Light Orchestra

♥ ♣ ♦ ♠

THE WUSSIEST POKER SONGS

"Deal 'Em Again" by Christopher Cross

"Lay Your Money Down" by Bread

HOW TO RIFFLE YOUR CHIPS

Like poker itself, if you want to learn to do the chip riffle properly, you're going to need a lot of practice.

1. Start out with two equally-sized stacks of four or five chips. You can build up the amount of chips you use over time. Some people find it easier to start out on a softer surface like a firm pillow rather than on a table.

2. Assuming you're right-handed (reverse this if you're a lefty), place your index finger and your middle finger on the left side and your ring finger and your pinky on the right side.

3. Start your thumb off on the left side of the right stack, lifting it just a little bit as you push the stacks together.

4. As you lift, slide your thumb over to the right side of the right stack, to help push the two stacks into one.

5. Once the first few chips fall into place, the chips higher up will start to glide into place easily, creating a nice "riffle" effect.

SOME PERCENTAGES OF POTS WON WITH VARIOUS STARTING HANDS IN HOLD'EM

| | NO. OF OPPONENTS | | |
	1	5	9
A-A	85.3	49.2	35.1
A-Ksuited	67	31.1	20.7
A-Koffsuit	65.4	27.9	17.2
A-Qsuited	66.1	29.4	19.3
A-Qoffsuit	64.5	25.9	15.5
A-2offsuit	54.6	16.1	9.1
K-K	82.4	43	26.1
K-Qoffsuit	61.4	25.1	15.1
Q-Q	79.9	37.9	22.2
Q-7suited	54.5	19.2	12.1
Q-7offsuit	51.9	15.1	8.0
10-10	75.1	30.0	17.2
10-2offsuit	41.5	10.6	5.8
7-7	66.2	21.9	13.7
2-2	50.3	15.5	12.0
7-2offsuit	34.6	8.6	4.8

(These figures are derived from a simulation study done by Steve Brecher and were computed by measuring the performance of the indicated hand against a set number of random hands played to showdown.)

THE ODD COUPLE:
It's hard to imagine
another television
show where poker
is such a part of the
fabric. For people
born before 1975,
poker on TV invari-
ably conjures up images of Vinnie, Speed, Murray the
Cop, and, of course, Felix Unger and Oscar Madison
sitting around the table just outside those kitchen
blinds. It was Oscar who uttered the immortal words
"That's why they call it gammmmmbling."

DEADWOOD: Poker games in saloons have always been
staples of TV westerns like *Gunsmoke*, and especially
Maverick, but this show deserves a special mention.
Not only does it contain more profanity than any card
game we've ever attended, but in its first season it
recreated one of the more famous real-life poker
moments of all time: the death of Wild Bill Hickok.
Keith Carradine gave an excellent performance as the
gunfighter turned gambler, shot in the head while
holding aces and eights.

MAVERICK: The aforementioned *Maverick* (with James
Garner and later Roger Moore) was a show with an
Old West card sharp as its main character, so it must
take its rightful place on this list as well.

THE SOPRANOS: America's favorite mob family has seen
its share of good poker scenes, thanks to the game for
high rollers the Soprano family runs in northern Jersey.
We've seen the game held up, seen local family men

go bust, heard plenty of ribald jokes and eyed some good-looking sopresatta and mozzarella. However, the main fascination with the game on the *Sopranos* has to be the oddball celebrities who drop in, like David Lee Roth, Lawrence Taylor and Frank Sinatra, Jr., as themselves.

POLICE SQUAD!: This short-lived but much loved comedy featured a truly memorable poker game in the back room of a gym, as Leslie Nielsen's Lt. Frank Drebin went undercover to win the contract of up-and-coming fighter Buddy Briggs. The trademark absurd humor was in fine fettle, with Nielsen's nemesis even throwing a pair of fuzzy dice into the pot only to have to object: "No dice!"

THE SIMPSONS: Viewers have been treated to a few instances of Homer Simpson's poker prowess, but one moment stands out. When Homer joins the local Stonecutter's lodge (a thinly-veiled goof on the Masons), he finds himself suddenly running the show, as an odd birthmark somehow proves that he's the group's long-awaited divine leader. Guest Patrick Stewart as the local Stonecutter chief and the other lodge members (typical Springfield regulars like Lenny, Carl and Mr. Burns) all must kow-tow to Homer, even letting him win in Ping-Pong and poker. When Homer shows that he has nothing in his hand and should lose the pot, Stewart insists that Homer take down the pot with what he tells him is the extremely valuable hand-to-beat-all-other-hands, the "royal sampler."

POKER PROFILE: THE
TEXAS ROAD GAMBLERS

The now legendary Texas road gambler team of "Amarillo Slim" Preston, Doyle "Texas Dolly" Brunson, and Brian "Sailor" Roberts used to travel around the backroads of Texas looking for people brave (or stupid) enough to play poker with them. And it wasn't just poker, they'd take on all comers in any game where they felt they had an edge. Their real edge, of course, was booking sports, which they did until the Wire Act was passed in 1968. They stayed together for about six years, but eventually broke up shortly after their first trip to Las Vegas.

✺ BIOS ✺

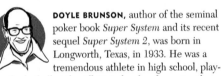

DOYLE BRUNSON, author of the seminal poker book *Super System* and its recent sequel *Super System 2*, was born in Longworth, Texas, in 1933. He was a tremendous athlete in high school, playing basketball at the All-State level and running the fastest mile in the Texas championships. After college, he was courted by the then-Minneapolis Lakers but a broken leg ended his basketball career. He kept his competitive fires burning by mastering the game of poker, which he'd learned to play in college at Hardin-Simmons University in Abilene. Doyle took to the road with Sailor and Slim and became one of the all-time greats. He was the first to win a $1 million poker tournament and overall he has netted nine World Series of Poker bracelets (including the Main Event title in 1976 and 1977). His nickname, Texas Dolly, comes from an incorrect reading of his name by Jimmy "The Greek" Snyder.

BRIAN "SAILOR" ROBERTS was a champion bridge player before he went on to poker glory. His generosity and love of chasing women are equally legendary – he was well-known for staking poker players who were down on their luck and he couldn't get enough of the nightlife. Sailor learned to gamble during his stint in the Navy, where he served in Korea, and earned his nickname. Roberts went on to win three World Series bracelets including the Main Event in 1975. He died from sclerosis related to hepatitis.

 AMARILLO SLIM PRESTON was born in Johnson, Arkansas, in 1928. He was a pool hustler before he was a poker player and won five Cadillacs as a teenager while serving in the Navy. Slim won the World Series of Poker in 1972 and went on to become poker's greatest ambassador. He appeared on *The Tonight Show* eleven times and even landed a part in Robert Altman's film, *California Split*. He's played poker against two U.S. Presidents, Richard Nixon and Lyndon Johnson. While playing in Colombia, he was kidnapped by drug lord Pablo Escobar but was later released.

For more information about Slim and the road gamblers, check out his memoir, written with Greg Dinkin in 2003, *Amarillo Slim in a World Full of Fat People* and the website http://www.thepokermba.com/amarilloslim.

"So one night, me and Doyle and Sailor stayed out all night at the racetrack, and we were riding down the highway from El Paso to Chihuahua. We made a pact that we weren't going to gamble among ourselves.

We had just entered into the edge of the Sierra Madre when Doyle started in, 'Slim, how long you think it'd take you to shimmy up the side of that mountain?'

I took a look and I said, 'Well, I could run up there before sundown.' Sailor wasn't convinced and said, 'Hell, you couldn't climb up there in two days.' Nothing more was said, until we saw a little bigger mountain down the road. Sailor said, 'Doyle, how long you think it would take you to shimmy up that mountain?' Doyle looked at it and he said, 'Oh, I could climb it in two hours.'

> "Get your fat ass out there," Sailor said, "it's a bet."

Sailor leaned over – now I was driving more than ninety miles an hour – shoved me over, and slammed on the brakes! 'Get your fat ass out there,' Sailor said, 'it's a bet.' I think they bet $2,000.

Doyle shimmied up there like a mountain goat on a mission. When he came on back down, Sailor refused to hand him that money; he just threw it on the floor-board of the car. And Doyle refused to pick it up. That money lay there for a long time, and I kept saying: 'No more gambling among ourselves on this here road trip.'"

Of course, by the time the trip was over, the three had made many more bets.

❤ ♣ ♦ ♠

ROBERT WILLIAMSON III ON COFFEE HOUSING (TABLE CHATTER)

 Mike Caro once said, "A fun game is a good game." If people are having a good time, they're not going to mind losing their money. So I try to create the most festive, fun atmosphere I can. I consider myself an entertainer. I'm there to entertain people. And in return, they pay me. They don't always realize they're paying me, but they're going to.

In the meantime, not only am I making sure that they're having a good time but I'm also gathering intelligence because they're giving away things about the strengths of their hands. So I'm really putting out feelers to gather information at the same time that I'm making sure that they're having a good time, which makes them want to keep playing with me. I have people that I've beaten for years that call me up and say, "Robert, where are you going to be in the next two weeks, I want to come play with you." I don't like to play with the top pros. I'm not looking for competition, I'm looking to win.

PHIL GORDON'S KEY TO
NO-LIMIT HOLD'EM SUCCESS

Phil Gordon, the poker analyst for *Celebrity Poker Showdown* and author, is one of the most respected and eloquent voices on NLH. Throughout the book, he'll share his thoughts on the most played game in the world.

SELECTIVE AGGRESSION: Most people can play an immediately passable game as long as they can master one concept – selective aggression. Be very selective about the hands that you play. Normally that means you're only going to play good cards. But when you choose to play you want to play aggressively. Be the player who bets and raises, not the player who checks and calls. If you can just master that one concept, you'll be able to play a passable game.

BET AND RAISE: Betting and raising gives you two ways to win: either you can have the best hand or your opponent can fold. When you just check or call, the only way you're going to win is to have the best hand. Having that extra way to win is absolutely vital. If you think about poker, there's always a right and a wrong decision to make. For instance, let's say we're playing one-on-one, and both of us turn over our cards. If I bet and you have the best hand, you're going to raise. If I bet and you have the worst hand, you're going to fold. Calling is never right. If you could see your opponents' cards, you'd always raise or you'd always fold. When you play aggressive poker, you're applying that concept. Another advantage of betting and raising is that it gives you more information about what other players are likely to be holding. If you allow everyone to just limp in, you have no idea where they are and where you stand.

Since your opponent is not going to play his hand face up, you need to discern what he or she is holding. This can be done by following a simple mental script.

> **I ask myself:** Do I think I have the best hand? If I think I have the best hand then I almost always raise or bet.
>
> **Then I ask:** Do I think I have the worst hand? If the answer to that question is yes, I almost always fold or check. In that situation I want to put as little money in the pot as possible.

It's only if I'm not sure if I have the best hand or the worst hand that I ever think about calling. Calling is always the last option. Raise if you've got the best hand, fold if you've got the worst hand and only call if you're really not sure.

POKER BOOKS BY PHIL GORDON

Poker: The Real Deal (written with Jonathan Grotenstein)

Phil Gordon's Little Green Book: Lessons and Teachings in No Limit Texas Hold'em

STATES WHERE POKER IS LEGAL

White areas indicate states where poker is legal in at least one place.

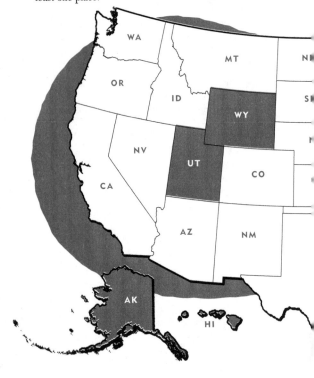

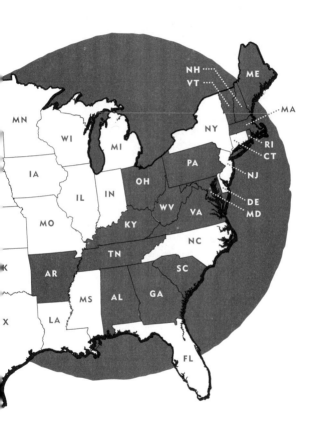

MN
WI
MI
NY
NH
VT
ME
MA
RI
CT
NJ
PA
OH
DE
MD
IA
IL
IN
WV
VA
MO
KY
NC
TN
SC
AR
AL
GA
MS
LA
FL

The World Series found the boost that it needed from an unlikely source: a book. It was Doyle Brunson who paved the way for the event – and the game – to make its mark. *Doyle Brunson's Super System: A Course in Power Poker* inspired a new breed of players to play. By teaching players how to play the odds and use aggression to their advantage, *Super System* became a treasure map to the World Series' pot of gold.

"It really democratized the game, really set the stage for others to come in," says Jonathan Grotenstein, co-author (with Storms Reback) of the book *All In*, about the history of the World Series of Poker, due out this fall from Thomas Dunne Books. "All of a sudden this new breed came along that studied books on poker, learned the odds and got very good very quickly."

The prevailing attitude soon became: "If that guy can do it, why can't I?"

Bobby Baldwin quickly became the poster child for this generation of poker whiz kids. A 20-something University of Oklahoma product who'd already impressed with wins in three WSOP events in 1977, Baldwin knocked off many of the game's heavyweights to capture the Main Event in 1978.

The WSOP's growth quickly caught fire. Binion's annual goal was to ensure the number of entrants and total prize money rose every year, so that no one would doubt the World Series' status as the biggest poker happening in the world. To that end, the late '70s brought the start of satellite events, designed to fill the tournament's slots with players from across the country and around the world. Players who couldn't afford or simply didn't want to pay the $10,000 entry fee could challenge other players on a smaller stage for $1,000, with the winner claiming a seat in the Main Event. The satellite system paid rapid dividends, as the World Series declined in size just once in its history, between the 1991 and 1992 events.

Another push occurred a year after Baldwin's dramatic win. In 1979 Hal Fowler, a public relations rep from Los Angeles, went on a wild run of amazing luck. Considered one of the worst players in WSOP history, Fowler pushed all-in again and again throughout the tournament, winning draw after draw, often with miracle cards. The story held that he did so while popping 20 quaaludes during the Main Event. When Fowler beat seasoned pro Bobby Haas to win the $270,000 first prize, poker wannabes from all over took notice. "It was horrible for Bobby Haas, but great for the Horseshoe," Grotenstein says.

Indeed, the prevailing attitude soon became: "If that guy can do it, why can't I?" Attendance at the WSOP jumped by 30 entrants between 1979 and 1980. Where the early events had been dominated by road gamblers from Texas, the event was now suddenly open to a wider audience. Rather than go through the poker school of hard knocks the way Moss, Brunson and others had, younger players could take their seat with the big boys. With the math element down cold, they figured they needed only to master the guile and nuances required to win the big prize. (The next segment on WSOP history starts on page 132.)

JOHNNY MOSS
(1907-1997)

Without Johnny Moss, high-stakes Las Vegas poker would not be what it is today. He won three World Series of Poker championships – and the tournament didn't exist until he was 63 years old!

At the age of 10 in Odessa, Texas, Moss played his first game of cards. As a teen he learned the tricks of the trade, like marking cards and bottom dealing. But Moss was no cheater. He employed his knowledge for a good cause: keeping the game honest. Moss was hired as a teenager by local saloons to keep his eye on the tables and the game clean – soon the hours of observation gave him keen insight into the hearts and minds of players.

Upon losing his last pot, before retiring to bed, the Greek stood from the table and uttered the now-famous words, "Mr. Moss, I have to let you go."

Moss played in the saloons and high-stakes private games of Texas and the South, traveling less than his peers (the famed Texas road gambler team of Doyle Brunson, Amarillo Slim and Sailor Roberts). One day, during a marathon session lasting several days, Johnny received a phone call. It was his boyhood friend and casino owner Benny Binion inviting him to participate in what would become poker's most famous challenge. In 1949, Moss packed his bags and flew to Las Vegas for the first time.

Nick "The Greek" Dandalos, a gambling man of immeasurable wealth, asked Binion to match him against "any man around" in a no-limit, no-holds-barred, winner-take-all heads up poker marathon. Moss got off the plane, hopped into a cab and sat down at a table in Binion's Horseshoe Club for the game of his life. Moss and Dandalos played almost continuously in public view for five months, sleeping only once every four or five days. Fresh dealers were rotated in every 20 minutes. In the end, after trading $500,000 pots back and forth, Moss wore the Greek down and won "the biggest game in town," estimated between $2 and 4 million. Upon losing his last pot, before retiring to bed, the Greek stood from the table and uttered the now-famous words, "Mr. Moss, I have to let you go."

Moss stayed in Las Vegas and was a successful pro for many years. He went on to win the World Series of Poker (an event in part inspired by his legendary battle with Nick "The Greek") in three of its first four years, 1970, 1971 and 1974. He died in 1997 in Las Vegas.

RULES FOR LOWBALL GAMES

LOWBALL: Basic Lowball is just like Five-Card Draw except you're trying to get the best possible low hand instead of the best possible high hand. There's no qualified low because there's no split pot – the low takes the whole pot. It's easier to get a pat hand in Lowball, which brings bluffing into the game a little more.

RAZZ: Razz is Seven-Card Stud played for the low. The betting structure and rounds mimic regular Seven-Card Stud but the object is to have the lowest possible hand, a la Lowball. Usually, the wheel is the best low hand and straights and flushes don't count against you.

♥ ♣ ♦ ♠

THE RANK OF HANDS FOR LOW

The value of low hands is measured from the top down.

> **1.** 5-4-3-2-A *(wheel)*
>
> **2.** 6-4-3-2-A
>
> **3.** 6-5-3-2-A
>
> **4.** 6-5-4-2-A
>
> **5.** 6-5-4-3-2
>
> **6.** 7-4-3-2-A
>
> **7.** 7-5-3-2-A etc.

This is the most common ranking and in this system, straights and flushes don't count against the low. But beware. It's important that before you play any Lowball game, you understand which hand is lowest. In the chart above, wheel low is the best low. But to some players, the wheel, also being a straight, is not considered a low hand at all. For these folks, 6-4-3-2-A is the lowest hand. And then there's Kansas City Lowball, where the ace is always high and the lowest hand is 7-5-4-3-2. Flushes also count against you. This is also known as Deuce-to-Seven Lowball and is a staple at the World Series of Poker.

QUALIFIED LOW

In many high-low split games, to win the low you need to have a hand with at least an eight high or lower. Omaha High-Low Split is always played this way. You'll often see Seven-Card Stud played without a qualifier. Whichever method you choose, just make sure you're clear on the rules from the get-go.

A SHORT RANT ABOUT CHECK RAISING

<RANT ON> For some unacceptable reason, there's an old-school line of thought that check raising – checking and then raising later in the same round – is at best a breach of poker etiquette and at worst something that is made illegal/outlawed altogether. Supposedly, the logic is that in a game among friends it's somehow inappropriate to "sandbag" or indicate you have a weak hand by checking only to later raise after another player bets. In reality, this goes against everything poker is supposed to be about: sure, check raising is deceptive but so is bluffing! Eliminate deception from poker and you might as well be playing War for crissakes. Any player in your game who suggests eliminating check-raising should be ignored, unless it comes from the host in which case you do what he says and immediately look for a new game once this one is over. </END OF RANT>

THE BEST OF THE POKER BLOGS

♥ ♣ ♦ ♠

GUINNESS AND POKER: HEADQUARTERS
FOR POKER NEWS ON THE WEB
http://www.guinnessandpoker.blogspot.com

Dubbed "The Blogfather" by his peers, Iggy offers
links to daily poker news articles, notable tidbits from
assorted poker message boards and highlights from
recent poker blog updates, brought to you with his
unique wit and wisdom (and a six-pack of Guinness).

♥ ♣ ♦ ♠

THE CARDS SPEAK: THE THINKING
PERSON'S POKER BLOG
http://cardsspeak.servebeer.com

Known for his thoughtful posts on poker theory, author
HDouble chronicles the psychological and personal
aspects of a developing poker player.

♥ ♣ ♦ ♠

LION TALES: A TOURNAMENT PROFESSIONAL'S
QUEST FOR WORLD POKER STARDOM
http://www.brodietech.com/liontales/blog.htm

Lion Tales offers insight into the world of high stakes
tournament poker, chronicling one man's quest to
make it to the final table on the World Poker Tour.

♥ ♣ ♦ ♠

POKER GRUB: A PROFESSIONAL GAMBLER'S TALES
OF EARNING BREAD AT THE POKER TABLE
http://www.pokergrub.com

Playwright and gambler Grubby offers humorous tales
of making a living as a poker player in Las Vegas.

POKER WORKS: BELLAGIO DEALER OFFERS A
VIEW FROM THE OTHER SIDE OF THE TABLE
http://pokerworks.com/blog/blogger.html

One of the original poker bloggers, Linda offers readers a rare glimpse into the highest limit poker games on the planet from the dealer's perspective.

♥ ♣ ♠ ♦

UP FOR POKER: A JOURNALIST, NEWS ANCHOR,
AND LOW-LIMIT GURU TALK POKER
http://www.upforanything.net/poker

Up for Poker's three contributors bring a little bit of everything to the table. Main-man Otis brings a background in journalism, and his superb writing covers topics from illegal home games in Missouri garages to the way that fatherhood has affected his poker game.

♥ ♣ ♠ ♦

CHRIS HALVERSON: AN UP-AND-COMING
POKER PLAYER DESCRIBES THE LOW-LIMIT GRIND
http://www.chrishalverson.com

Known for his obsession with collecting free money from online poker bonuses, Chris dissects the low-limit games with his analytical mind.

♥ ♣ ♠ ♦

DOUBLEAS: INSIDE THE MIND OF A
GREAT NO-LIMIT PLAYER
http://doubleas.blogspot.com

DoubleAs rigorously breaks down his thinking during difficult hands in medium-stakes no-limit games. His explanation of the decision-making process at the table is both entertaining and instructive.

JOHN VORHAUS ON ONLINE POKER

In addition to Poker Night *(pg. 22), John Vorhaus is also the author of the* Killer Poker *series, including* Killer Poker Online. *Here are his Dos and Don'ts of online poker.*

DON'Ts

DON'T play big. Online poker is great but you don't want to put a lot of money into it because there are just too many pitfalls. For one, the pace of play is just so fast that if there are any holes in your game at all, they will be greatly magnified. It's easy to lose money fast but it's not so easy to win money fast.

DON'T be distracted. Online poker can encourage incorrect play. Just because you can play at home while watching TV, talking on the phone and feeding the dog all at the same time doesn't mean you should. You will be punished for any lack of concentration.

DON'T succumb to OMHS (one more hand syndrome). You need to have an exit strategy. It's very easy to reward yourself for having a good day by playing a few hands of online poker. The next thing you know it's 4 A.M. One reason that tournaments online are a good idea is that when one is over, you need to make a conscious decision to play in another one. It's easier to avoid the trap of playing in "one more hand."

DOs

DO be ruthlessly honest with yourself. Almost everybody loses in online poker. This is no different than any other poker environment but it's made worse by three factors: the speed of play, the phenomenon of chair glue (an object at the poker table tends to stay at the poker table unless acted upon by an outside force) and gamnesia (an uncanny ability that certain gamblers have to forget what they've lost).

DO take advantage of the chance to analyze your play. Between the hand histories available on many online sites and resources like http://www.pokercharts.com, you can much more easily get a detailed look in the mirror online than you can in a live game.

DO use the chat box appropriately. You never want to reveal your psychic pain in a chat box. These conversations can turn ugly and cause distraction. Make sure to avoid them. Instead, you should calmly and consciously try to put a susceptible opponent on tilt. Otherwise, avoid the chat box altogether.

DO find the fish. Between all the stats available at many online sites and your own ability to make notes about other players, you can really use game selection to your advantage online. You want to pay attention to the average number of players at the table, the average number of players who see the flop and the number of hands dealt per hour. Ideally, you want a game with a full table that plays swiftly, with a lot of players seeing the flop, but not a lot of players raising. The goal is to play against weak, passive, predictable players as often as possible.

POKER ETIQUETTE: WHAT NOT TO DO

These are things that are considered bad poker etiquette. The host has license to issue a warning, enforce a penalty paid to the pot or even bar someone if any of these behaviors persist.

PLAYING OUT OF TURN: It's extremely important that you wait until your turn to check, call, raise or fold. It's unfair to give away any additional information about your hand to the players who have yet to act.

STRING RAISING: A string raise occurs when you first call and then raise an opponent. While traditionally not uncommon in home games, "I'll see your nickel and raise you a quarter!," string raises aren't good poker etiquette and can lead to disputes. This is particularly the case when they are deliberately used in an attempt to proffer undue information about your opponent's hand by trying to read their reaction after you say "see" or "call."

SPLASHING THE POT: Your chips should be neatly placed into the pot, not thrown in haphazardly. This is so your opponents can see how much you're putting in and to verify that you don't short the pot.

REVEALING YOUR CARDS BEFORE THE HAND IS OVER: As with acting out of turn, volunteering information about your hand is bad poker manners, whether you're still alive in the hand or you have folded.

COMMENTING ON POSSIBLE HANDS: This entails looking at the board and saying something like, "Hey, look, there's three diamonds showing, maybe somebody has a flush!"

SLOW ROLLING: Acting as though you've been beaten and then revealing a winning hand is pretty much the poker equivalent of doing an endzone dance and pretending to moon the crowd.

STALLING: It's one thing to take a second to consider the pot odds or give yourself a minute before calling an all-in raise, but in general your goal should be to keep things moving swiftly and keep with the flow of play.

USING ABUSIVE LANGUAGE TO THE OTHER PLAYERS OR DEALER: This is really bad form and will definitely come back to haunt you, by hurting your karma or getting you beat up in the parking lot.

TALKING ON YOUR WIRELESS PHONE AT THE TABLE: Do us all a favor and step outside if you need to talk on the phone.

♥ ♦ ♣ ♠

THE ODDS AGAINST SEEING AN OVERCARD WHEN YOU HAVE A POCKET PAIR IN HOLD'EM

K-K	23%	3.4-1
Q-Q	41%	1.4-1
J-J	57%	.75-1
10-10	70%	.44-1
9-9	79%	.26-1
8-8	87%	.15-1
7-7	92%	.09-1
6-6	96%	.04-1
5-5	98%	.02-1
4-4	99.4%	.006-1
3-3	99.9%	.001-1

(these appear courtesy of http://www.pokersavvy.com)

PRE FLOP ODDS

The odds against getting two suited cards **3.25-1**
The odds against getting A-K, suited or unsuited **82-1**
The odds against getting A-K, suited **330-1**
The odds against getting any pocket pair **16-1**
The odds against getting any specific pocket pair **220-1**

♥ ♣ ♦ ♠

THE FLOP AND BEYOND

The odds against flopping a set, full-house or quads when holding a pocket pair **7.5-1**

The odds against flopping at least two of your suit when you hold two suited cards **6.4-1**

The odds against flopping a flush **118-1**

The odds against flopping a straight when holding any two connecting cards, 4-5 through J-10 .... **76-1**

The odds against making a backdoor flush, runner-runner when holding two suited cards and one matching suit hits on the flop **23-1**

(odds courtesy of http://www.pokersavvy.com)

NICKNAMES FOR LOUSY PLAYERS

FISH	DONOR
LIVE ONE	PIGEON
ATM	MORK

NICKNAMES FOR TEXAS HOLD'EM HANDS

A-A: Rockets; American Airlines; Alcoholics Anonymous; Bullets

K-K: Cowboys; King Kong

Q-Q: Canadian Rockets; Canadian Aces; Siegfried & Roy; Ladies; Four Tits; Jailhouse Rock

J-J: Fishhooks; Hooks; Dyn-O-Mite

T-T: Double Dereks; Boxcars; Dimes

9-9: Phil Hellmuth; Wayne Gretzky, or Great Ones; Love Potion

9-2: Twiggy

8-8: Snowmen; Little Oldsmobile; Infinity and Beyond; Dog Balls; Racetracks

7-7: Walking Sticks; Hockey Sticks; Mullets; Sunset Strip

7-2: Beer Hand

6-6: Route 66; Kicks; Satan's Starter Set

5-5: Speed Limit; Nickels; Presto

4-5: Colt 45; Billy Dee Williams

4-4: Midlife Crisis; Sailboats; Magnum; Canadian Presto

3-3: Crabs; Larry Bird

2-2: Deuces; Ducks; Question Marks; Pocket Swans; Barely Legal

A-K: Big Slick

A-Q: Big Chick

A-J: Ajax, Blackjack

A-T: Johnny Moss

A-3: Ashtray

A-2: Little Slick

K-QSUITED: Marriage

K-QOFFSUIT: Mixed Marriage

K-J: Kojak

K-9: Canine, Fido

Q-J: Oedipus

Q-7: Computer Hand

Q-5: Grannie Mae

Q-3: Gay Waiter; San Francisco Busboy

J-5: Jackson Five; Motown

J-4: Flat Tire

T-8: Golden Dan

T-5: Woolworth's; Five and Dime

T-4: Broderick Crawford, The Good Buddy

T-2: Doyle Brunson

9-8: Oldsmobile

9-5: Dolly Parton, Hard Working Man

7-6: Union Oil

6-9: Big Lick; Dinner for Two

6-9s: Prom Night

5-7: Heinz

3-A: Baskin-Robbins

3-9: Jack Benny

3-8: Raquel Welch

3-3: Crabs

3-2: Mississippi Slick

2-2: Ducks

ASHLEY ADAMS' BEGINNING
STRATEGY FOR SEVEN-CARD STUD

Ashley Adams is the author of Winning 7-Card Stud, *a book endorsed by Doyle Brunson, Mike Caro and World Poker Tour commentator Mike Sexton. Here are his keys for success at Seven-Stud, assuming low limits and a loose-passive game (a game where there are a lot of players entering the pot and just calling).*

✳ STARTING HAND PLAY ✳

You're only going to want to play four types of hands after the first three cards are dealt:

- Three-of-a-kind
- A pair
- Three to a flush
- Three to a straight

✳ PLAY THE HIGH PAIR AGGRESSIVELY ✳

You'll want to play the low pair sparingly and with a good kicker or you can play it if you have good position (if you're one of the last players to act).

Only play the three-flush if there aren't more than two of your suit out (showing elsewhere on the table).

Be very careful when playing the three-straight. Obviously, high three-straights are better than low ones. Gapped three-straights aren't worth playing at all.

Always take your position into account when making your play. The more players who act before you, the better.

❧ FOURTH STREET ❧

If you have the best hand at this stage, play it aggressively.

Fold if someone else has a pair showing.

If you were drawing to a straight or flush and the fourth card didn't help, fold.

❧ FIFTH STREET ❧

Again, if it looks like you have the best hand, continue to play aggressively.

If you are on a draw and your cards are very live (the ones you need haven't been seen elsewhere), go ahead and call.

If you are on a draw and your cards are not very live, fold.

❧ SIXTH STREET ❧

In general on sixth street, if it looks like another player might have a hand that you can't beat even if you hit your hand on the river, fold to a bet. If you think you're in the lead, you should bet. And if you're on a draw and your hand is likely to best if you hit it, you should call.

❧ THE RIVER ❧

Call on the river unless you're certain you're beat – there's so much money in the pot at that point that your odds when you call are almost certain to be right.

Check if you're unsure of where you stand.

Bet with your hand if there's even a slight chance that your opponent will call you with an inferior hand.

ASHLEY ADAMS' DOS AND DON'TS FOR YOUR FIRST CASINO POKER GAME

DOs

DO take fifteen to thirty minutes when you arrive at a casino to consider your game and what your plan of action will be.

DO think about how you are playing as opposed to whether you are up or down.

DO stick to your strategy whether you are up or down.

DO evaluate your session immediately after you have finished playing.

DO stop playing when you've lost more than you can handle psychologically.

DON'Ts

DON'T expect to win the first time you sit down.

DON'T be intimidated by others or change your play to enhance your image.

DON'T be distracted by other players' mannerisms.

DON'T assume that other players are good just because they appear comfortable and talk a lot.

DON'T assume that you'll be able to win just because you've read a book.

DON'T rush into playing when you first arrive.

DON'T continue to play if you're distracted in any way (hungry, tired, angry, too far down, even too far up).

SOME ONLINE HANDLES

ACECRACK	EFFENRIVER	MORECOWBELL
AMARILLOFATS	EMPTYSEAT88	NUTSRGOOD
BLUFFSWITH72	FISHGOBBLER	TAYKINURMONEY
CANIWINAHAND	FTHERAKE	TILTSALOT
CHASETILRIVR	I_AM_DRUNK	TOOMANYTELLS
CHEWBACCA	IGOTTAFLUSH	UAREALLFISH
CMONEYMACKER	IH8RVRRATS	URAISEIFOLD
DEAD$MONEY	INEEDADATE	USUALLYBLUFFING
DEEZNUTZ	LUVTHENUTS	WHAMROCKS
EATMYNUTZ	MEWANTYMONEY	WHERESMYSTACK

OTHER/FORMER PROFESSIONS OF PROFESSIONAL POKER PLAYERS

Accountant. . . . . Chris Moneymaker

Attorney . . . . Dan Harrington

Pro Soccer Player . . . . David Levi

Hair Stylist . . . . Mel Judah

Magician . . . . Antonio Esfandiari

Go-Go Bar Owner . . . . Vince Burgio

Actor. . . . . Ross Boatman

Lifeguard . . . . Chip Jett

Chip Shop Owner . . . . Peter Costa

CFL Player . . . . T.J. Cloutier

Air Traffic Controller . . . . John Cernuto

Music Promoter . . . . Paul Darden

Repo Man . . . . Phil Laak

PHIL GORDON'S KEYS TO NO-LIMIT SUCCESS, PART 2

POSITION: Position is another incredibly important factor. Having your opponent act before you gives you a tremendous amount of information. It allows you to apply that script I was talking about on page 87 in a more straightforward way. After they act, you have additional information about whether you have the best hand or the worst hand. If they check, then you probably have a much greater chance of having the best hand so you can bet. If you bet, that gives you several other pieces of information to deal with: How did they bet, aggressively or tentatively? How much did they bet? Why did they bet? Then you apply those answers to the question of whether or not you have the best hand.

Also, when they're out of position, they have to commit chips to the pot before you have to commit any. The edge of being in position is just monstrous. The other thing that people don't realize is that it's much tougher to flop a good hand than people think. For instance, let's say you have A-K or A-Q or A-J or any of those type of unpaired cards. You're only going to flop a pair about 34% of the time. That means that 66% of the time – two out of every three attempts – you're going to miss the flop completely. Now, when I'm in position that means I should win when I hit the flop and most of the times that your opponent doesn't!

> The other thing that people don't realize is that it's much tougher to flop a good hand than people think.

PHIL GORDON ON GAME SELECTION

In cash games, game selection is everything. The old expression, "If you look around the table and you can't see the sucker, it's you," well, that's game selection. Even an OK player is going to win money if he or she is playing with worse players. That said, you don't have to be the best player at the table to win money. All you've got to do is be better than two or three of your opponents at the table and the game can still be profitable in No-Limit. Most of the money that's won in No-Limit comes from two or three players at the table. At the top level it only takes one sucker to make the game profitable. Either that or the pros are just trading money back and forth, waiting for the sucker to come to the game. If you see Johnny Chan and Gus Hansen and Barry Greenstein sitting down at the table together, they're not sitting down together because they think they have an advantage over each other. They're sitting down in the hope that a guy with a suitcase full of money from Mobile, Alabama, is going to sit down at the table with them.

> Even an OK player is going to win money if he or she is playing with worse players.

♥ ♦ ♣ ♠

NICKNAMES FOR OMAHA HANDS

A-K-4-7: Machine Gun

K-K-K-K: The Four Horsemen

J-J-5-5: Jackson Five

T-T-T-X: Thirty Miles of Bad Road

3-3-2-2: Socks and Shoes

LITERARY QUOTES
ABOUT CARDS/POKER

"One of these days in your travels, a guy is going to come up to you and show you a nice brand-new deck of cards on which the seal is not yet broken, and this guy is going to offer to bet you that he can make the jack of spades jump out of the deck and squirt cider in your ear. But, son, do not bet this man, for as sure as you are standing there, you are going to end up with an earful of cider."

–Damon Runyon

"I must complain the poker cards are ill-shuffled till I have a good hand."

–Jonathan Swift

"Poker's the only game fit for a grown man. Then, your hand is against every man's, and every man's is against yours."

–W. Somerset Maugham

"He was about to gamble his life on that poker table, and the insanity of that risk filled him with a kind of awe."

–Paul Auster

"There are few things that are so unpardonably neglected in our country as poker. The upper class knows very little about poker. Now and then you find ambassadors who have sort of a general knowledge of poker, but the ignorance of the people is fearful. Why, I have known clergymen, good men, kind-hearted, liberal, sincere, and all that, who did not know the meaning of a 'flush.' It is enough to make one ashamed of the species."

–Mark Twain

"Many bad players will not improve because they cannot bear self-knowledge."

–David Mamet

(Derived from *Poker Aces: The Stars of Tournament Poker* by Ron Rose)

♥ ♣ ♦ ♠

BARRY GREENSTEIN IS A VERY GOOD LISTENER

 Through the years, Barry Greenstein has picked up a passing knowledge of Vietnamese, at least when it comes to poker. When he first started playing with fellow WSOP champion and Vietnam native Chau Giang, he'd chat with him about various hands in Chau's native tongue. But given that Barry's vocabulary in Vietnamese was about the same as a five-year-old's, when Chau would speak quickly most of what he said flew over Barry's head. One time Chau was explaining a subtle rule in a new game to the casino where they both played. Chau got frustrated at Barry's complete lack of comprehension. Barry's girl-friend went up to Chau and in fluent Vietnamese told him, "He doesn't understand you."

Chau was even more perplexed. "I've been talking to him in Vietnamese for three days."

She explained, "He's a very good listener."

THE BEST ACTION SPOTS IN THE USA

In the winter of 2004-2005, Jay Greenspan took a cross-country poker journey, playing any place he could find as he drove across the country. His book, Hunting Fish *(St. Martin's Press), chronicles the journey and is a book you want to read. Here are some of the best games he found along the way.*

BEST 5-10 NO-LIMIT GAME

Grand Casino, Biloxi, MS: This game only goes once or twice a month, usually on Saturdays. But it is worth the wait No draw is too unlikely, no bet too large to keep players from tossing chips into the pot. Play with a bib, as drool is sure to form when you see how juicy this game is.

BEST OMAHA HIGH/LOW GAME

Village Club, Chula Vista, CA (outside of San Diego): Village Club is as seedy and angry a cardroom as you're likely to encounter. Arguments are common, as are drunks. It seemed folding in the Omaha high/low game there was viewed as some sort of moral failure. The pots are so large as to be surreal.

BEST SPOT TO FLEECE THE COUNTRY-CLUB SET

Houston, TX: Houston is crazy about two activities: golf and poker. On days when the lawyers and entrepreneurs aren't at the links, they're splashing money around at a poker table. Mention Ernie Els and they seem happy enough to hand over piles of cash.

BEST ACTION SPOT IN THE USA

Tunica, MS, in January: When the World Poker Tour rolls into Tunica, poker players from all over the South and Midwest flock to this town 30 minutes from Memphis. The action at all levels, from 1-2 No-Limit Hold'em to 50-100 Pot-Limit Omaha, is fantastic. The rooms are cheap, the food is comped and the games are wide open. If you don't mind the dearth of non-poker activities, you're sure to enjoy Tunica.

♥ ♣ ♦

POKER PHRASES THAT HAVE ENTERED THE LEXICON

ACE IN THE HOLE

BEATS ME

BLUE CHIP

CALL YOUR BLUFF

CASH IN

PASS THE BUCK

PLAY THE CARDS YOU'RE DEALT

PLAYING YOUR CARDS CLOSE TO YOUR VEST

POKER FACE

STACK UP

UP THE ANTE

WHEN THE CHIPS ARE DOWN

WILD CARD

SOME FAMOUS POKER HANDS

DOYLE BRUNSON: Brunson won both his World Series of Poker Main Events with the same hand, 10-2. It's been called by his name ever since.

THE COMPUTER HAND: There's a lot of disagreement over the exact etymology of this phrase but everyone agrees that the hand is Q-7 offsuit. In some places it's referred to as simply the median of all potential starting hands. Other places claim that the name comes from (a likely apocryphal) computer study where it was determined to be the worst starting hand that was still profitable to play – a dubious claim at best. The term has also come to mean a hand that a computer simulation deems as correct to play that in reality is not.

7-2 OFFSUIT: The worst starting hand you can get in Hold'em because there are no straights or flushes that can be made using both cards.

THE BOSS LEEGAY: A leegay is any hold'em hand that doesn't contain an ace, two suited cards or two connected cards – basically an unplayable hand. The best possible leegay is K-8 offsuit and it's also called the boss leegay. The hold'em games in Southern California were so soft in the early '90s that a few of the pros would judge the quality of a game based on the number of "leegays" that were shown down on the river.

VARKONYI'S Q-10: At the 2002 World Series of Poker, Robert Varkonyi knocked out Phil Hellmuth with an unusual hand, Q-10. But that's not what made the hand famous. Hellmuth, doing commentary on ESPN post-knockout, declared that if Varkonyi went on to win the tournament, he'd get his head shaved, pro-wrestling style. With four players left at the final table,

Varkonyi put away Scott Gray with another Q-10. Shortly after, it came down to Varkonyi against Julian Gardner. Gardner went all-in with J♣ 8♣, Varkonyi called with, you guessed it, Q-10! The board came Q♣ 4♣ 4♦ 10♠, meaning that the result would all hinge on the river. When it came up 10♣, Gardner had made the flush but it didn't matter because Varkonyi beat him with an improbable full house to win the World Series of Poker! Hellmuth took his punishment like a man.

THE DEAD MAN'S HAND: Aces and eights, the hand that Wild Bill Hickok was holding when he was shot in the back, remains the most referenced poker hand of all time.

MEMBERS OF THE POKER HALL OF FAME
ALONG WITH YEAR OF INDUCTION

JOHNNY MOSS 1979	WALTER CLYDE "PUGGY" PEARSON 1987
NICK "THE GREEK" DANDOLOS 1979	DOYLE BRUNSON 1988
FELTON "CORKY" MCCORQUODALE 1979	JACK "TREETOP" STRAUS . . .1988
RED WINN 1979	FRED "SARGE" FERRIS 1989
SID WYMAN 1979	BENNY BINION 1990
"WILD BILL" HICKOK 1979	"CHIP" REESE 1991
EDMOND HOYLE 1979	"AMARILLO SLIM" PRESTON . . .1992
T. "BLONDIE" FORBES 1980	JACK KELLER 1993
BILL BOYD 1981	"LITTLE MAN" POPWELL 1996
TOM ABDO 1982	ROGER MOORE 1997
JOE BERNSTEIN 1983	STU UNGAR 2001
MURPH HARROLD 1984	LYLE BERMAN 2002
RED HODGES 1985	JOHNNY CHAN 2002
HENRY GREEN 1986	BOBBY BALDWIN 2003
	BERRY JOHNSTON 2004

WAYS TO CHEAT

TRICK SHUFFLES: One rudimentary example of a trick shuffle is given on page 72 but there are many more impressive and elegant ways to place cards in the deck through sleight of hand. A skilled mechanic – card cheat – will have the ability to set the deck in nearly any way he wants through techniques like the over-hand tumble, jab shuffle or fan shuffle.

BOTTOM DEALING: While holding the deck to deal, the cheater peeks at the bottom card. If it's of use to him, he deals it to him or his partner. If not, it goes in order or to the hand that might be developing into a threat.

MARKING THE CARDS: A less-skilled mechanic is likely to have sharp fingernails that he'll use to leave nearly imperceptible dots or other marks on the cards so he'll recognize them later in the night and use that knowledge to his advantage.

CALLING YOUR HAND WRONG: This one's for serious amateur cheats only. Say you have a four flush in Five-Card Draw. You claim you have a flush at showdown and try to tuck that renegade club beneath your four spades. If you get caught you just apologize profusely and blame the alcohol.

SHORTING THE POT: Another oldie and not so goodie, when you short the pot, you fail to put in the correct number of chips. This is often accomplished by tossing your chips in the center haphazardly, aka, "splashing the pot."

WORKING WITH A PARTNER: Through various signals (given through hand motion, throat clearing or chip-stacking) it's fairly easy to let your partner in crime know exactly what you're holding. This extra knowledge, as well as the ability to trap a third party, gives a huge edge to the cheats. Partners also have the advantage of being able to pass cards to each other.

(Thanks to Andy Bellin's *Poker Nation* for providing the source material for much of this section.)

WAYS TO THWART CHEATING

▸▸ Require all the players to keep their cards above the table at all times.

▸▸ Always start the night with two new standard decks of cards. Any player in the game should be allowed to request a new deck at any time.

▸▸ Use a "shoe" (plastic card) or just tape the two jokers together and have the dealer hold them over the bottom of the deck to prevent peaking – though be warned a good mechanic will not be deterred by this.

▸▸ Be in tune to the sound of the cards. Cards dealt properly barely make any sound at all. The ones being dealt off the bottom of the deck tend to come out with more of a scraping sound.

▸▸ Be on the lookout for players dealing with an unusual grip. Holding the deck at too much of an angle or not lifting one's thumb off the top of the deck are signs that something fishy might be going on.

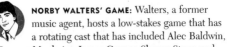

SOME WELL-KNOWN
HOLLYWOOD HOME GAMES

 NORBY WALTERS' GAME: Walters, a former music agent, hosts a low-stakes game that has a rotating cast that has included Alec Baldwin, Camryn Manheim, James Garner, Sharon Stone and Scott "Joanie Loves Chachi" Baio. Seven-Card Stud only.

VINCE VAN PATTEN'S GAME: This roving game organized by the World Poker Tour commentator has a $1,000 buy-in.

 TOBEY MAGUIRE'S GAME: Tobey's game, held at his Hollywood Hills manse, has a $2,000 buy-in.

REAGAN SILBER'S "BILLIONAIRE BOYS" GAME: Poker pro Silber's game in Bel Air has a $10,000 buy-in. Regulars include Leonardo DiCaprio and Tobey Maguire.

 HANK AZARIA'S GAME: Every Sunday in Beverly Hills. Matthew Perry and Josh Malina are regulars.

JON LANDAU'S GAME: Monday nights in Sherman Oaks. David Schwimmer and various entertainment execs appear frequently.

PAUL MAZURSKY'S GAME: Actor/director Mazursky hosts one of Hollywood's longest-running games, which has included such luminaries as Elliot Gould, Leonard Nimoy and Richard Dreyfuss.

CHRIS MASTERSON AND LAURA PREPON'S GAME: The action rarely stops as Masterson (*Malcolm in the Middle*) and Prepon (*That '70s Show*) host a game at their Los Feliz home five nights a week!

THE GOURMET POKER CLUB: Chevy Chase, Barry Diller, Carl Reiner and Neil Simon are among those who meet once a month for food and cards.

DAVID SKLANSKY ON THE
NEW BREED OF POKER PLAYERS

Master poker player/author David Sklansky has long been considered one of the game's great teachers. As such, his books have been responsible for educating a significant chunk of the poker population. When asked what effect the presence of all the new blood in the game is having on the more experienced players, he said:

The new people, even the ones who are reading my books, are bad for the good players but good for the great players. Because they play a B- game and that's tough enough that the medium-sized pros who play maybe a B or a B+ game don't have any edge over them with the rake, but the A and A- players still have a significant edge over them. When you're playing in the higher games like I do, it's rare that you find absolutely terrible players. We make our money off mediocre players and the more mediocre players that come into the game, the better.

COMIC BOOK HEROES AND VILLAINS
BASED ON PLAYING CARDS

Batman arch-villain **THE JOKER**

The Justice League's foes **THE ROYAL FLUSH GANG**

Cosmic superhero **JACK OF HEARTS**

The X-Men's enemy **JACK O'DIAMONDS**

Ranma's nemesis **THE GAMBLING KING**

Captain Britain's adversary **THE QUEEN OF HEARTS**

Sexy showgirl turned super-heroine **ACE OF DIAMONDS**

POKER FACTIONS

THE HENDON MOB: A group of players who used to play in a regular game in Hendon, England, who've since started traveling the world as a poker team, playing in tournaments and accruing many wins and in-the-money finishes.

JOE BEEVERS	ROSS BOATMAN
BARNY BOATMAN	RAM VASWANI

THE CREW: A group of young poker-playing friends who travel, play and talk about the game together.

DUTCH BOYD	JOE BATHOLDI
BOBBY BOYD	DAVID SMYTH
TONY LAZAR	SCOTT FISCHMAN

TEAM FULL TILT: The group of pros who play at http://www.fulltiltpoker.com.

ANDY BLOCH	PHIL IVEY
CHRIS FERGUSON	JOHN JUANDA
PHIL GORDON	HOWARD LEDERER
CLONIE GOWEN	ERICK LINDGREN
JENNIFER HARMAN	ERIK SEIDEL

FIVE GREAT POKER NARRATIVES

Poker Face: A Girlhood Among Gamblers
by Katherine Lederer

*One of a Kind: The Rise and Fall of Stuey
"The Kid" Ungar* by Nolan Dalla and Peter Alson

Positively Fifth Street by James McManus

The Biggest Game in Town by A. Alvarez

Big Deal: One Year as a Professional Poker Player
by Anthony Holden

PREFLOP HEAD-TO-HEAD TEXAS HOLD'EM HAND ODDS

Knowing your odds of winning a hand is essential to any poker player's success. Here's a list of some common situations pitting different types of opposing starting hands against one another. The odds don't equal 100% as they don't include ties. Suited cards noted with an 's.' (Odds courtesy of twodimes.net)

HAND	ODDS OF WINNING	HAND	ODDS OF WINNING
PAIR VS. UNDERPAIR		**PAIR VS. LOWER SUITED CONNECTORS**	
A-A	80.1%	Q-Q	77.5%
VS.		VS.	
7-7	19.6%	7s-8s	22.2%
HIGHER SUITED CONNECTORS VS. LOWER SUITED CONNECTORS		**SUITED HIGH CARDS VS. UNSUITED HIGH CARDS**	
9-10s	62.3%	A-Ks	52.5%
VS.		VS.	
4-5s	36%	A-Ko	47.5%

SOME MORE PREFLOP HEAD-TO-HEAD TEXAS HOLD'EM HAND ODDS

A-A	88.0%	8-8	66.2%	K-K	87.0%
VS.		VS.		VS.	
7-2	11.6%	As-2s	33.4%	10-2	12.6%
A-A	92.0%	A-6	53.5%	A-K	64.0%
VS.		VS.		VS.	
A-K	6.8%	Ks-Qs	46.1%	6-9	35.7%
J-J	53.7%	As-Qs	50.1%	5-5	50.9%
VS.		VS.		VS.	
As-Ks	45.9%	2-2	49.3%	Ks-9s	48.5%

CHIP PROXIES: WHAT TO USE WHEN YOU DON'T HAVE POKER CHIPS

Sure, it's great to have the world's most ornate clay chips. But sometimes you'll get the urge to play a few rounds when all you've got are a few snack foods and knick-knacks lying around the house. That's when it's time to get creative and look for other ways to post antes and blinds.

PRETZELS: Small enough to collect bundles and make a dramatic all-in bet. Delicious enough to provide extra incentive to making an opponent's ante mysteriously disappear. Given their fragility, they'll discourage splashing the pot – always a good thing.

MATCHES: Pre: Even smaller than pretzels, you can fit dozens into your clenched fist as you curse your opponent silently for calling your bluff. Con: Tough to rip 'em out one at a time from the matchbook. Plus, poker is not much fun when the table, your house and all your friends burst into flames.

GUM: The variety of offerings makes for multiple denominations. Chiclets are 1s, foil-wrapped gum 2s, gumballs 5s, jawbreakers 10s, Big League Chew pouches 50s. Warning: Not recommended for room temperatures above 72 degrees or with previously pocketed gum.

THUMBTACKS: Small and lightweight, both pluses. They're color-coded, which will make you think twice about calling a two-green-tacks-bet off the flop with an inside straight draw. DO NOT pound your stack in anger if you want to avoid the emergency room.

HOUSEHOLD PESTS: Roach infestation got you down? Fear not. You can put those ugly critters to good use by making them part of the game, instead of just having them circle your friends skittering for stray pizza crumbs. Protective gloves recommended.

POGS: If you fell victim to this 1990s fad, you've probably got a shoebox-full long forgotten in the corner of your closet. Right size, right shape for wagering. If you've got a monster hand, it's a great opportunity to check-raise, then rub it in with: "Remember Alf? He's back…in pog form!"

BOTTLE CAPS: Small and flippable, well-suited for the serious no-limit freezeout or a short-handed game of Five-Card Draw. Denominations run from barely college drinking game-worthy Milwaukee's Best Light (1 cent) to delicious Brugse Tripel ($1,000). Added bonus of making your buddies drink the beers first to impair their judgment.

▼ ♦ ♦ ♦

POKER PLAYERS WHOSE NICKNAMES ARE PLACE NAMES

"Never play cards with a guy who has the same first name as a city."

–Coach Bobby Finstock (Jay Tarses) in *Teen Wolf*

"MIAMI" JOHN CERNUTO

"SYRACUSE" CHRIS TSIPRAILIDIS

HOWARD "TAHOE" ANDREW

"DAYTONA" TONY COUSINEAU

RANDY "HOMETOWN" HOLLAND

JIM "CINCINNATI KID" LESTER

"AMARILLO SLIM" PRESTON

DOYLE "TEXAS DOLLY" BRUNSON

PHIL GORDON'S SIX FAVORITE TRAVEL DESTINATIONS

In addition to being a master of the felt, Phil Gordon is an accomplished traveler, having visited over 50 countries on six continents. Here are a few of his favorite places, along with a brief description of why.

SWEDEN: The women!

SOUTHERN CHILE: The mountains, the fjords, the glaciers, the people. I really like the Chilean culture.

ETHIOPIA: Probably the most difficult place I've ever traveled but still one of the best. When I went, there hadn't been a lot of tourism. I went to some villages there where they'd never seen white people before.

VIETNAM: Like Ethiopia, another place that hadn't seen much tourism. It was great to be in a place that hadn't been overrun by tourists.

SOUTH AFRICA: Cape Town is just an amazing place. It's right on the cliffs and the ocean and it's just beautiful.

AUSTRALIA: Fantastic, sports-oriented outgoing people, real party animals. I just had a fantastic time. I rented a truck and drove around for six months. It was probably the most fun I've ever had.

PHIL GORDON'S BEST CELEBRITY POKER PLAYERS
BEN AFFLECK AND TOBEY MAGUIRE

They're aggressive, they're thoughtful, they know what they're doing. They've put in significant time at the table. They love the game, they've studied the game, they've played with the best players in the world. They've paid the price to learn but they're fantastic players. It doesn't matter that they're celebrities – they're poker players.

♥ ♣ ♦

OTHER CELEBS WITH GREAT POKER SKILLS

MENA SUVARI	HANK AZARIA
CHRIS MASTERSON	MIMI ROGERS

FIVE PLAYERS NAMED NGUYEN
SCOTTY NGUYEN
MEN "THE MASTER" NGUYEN
KIM "DRAGON LADY" NGUYEN
MINH NGUYEN
PHI NGUYEN

POKER SUPERSTITIONS:
THE BIZARRE RITUALS POKER PLAYERS
USE TO COURT LADY LUCK

Even the most mathematically-gifted poker players seem to fall victim to weird superstitions at the poker table. Get your pocket aces or nut-straights-on-the-flop cracked enough times and you'll soon be grasping for any talisman or ritual that may break your run of bad luck. Until we can confirm the existence of leprechauns, these routines will have to suffice:

HOARDING CHIP COLORS: Home games can vary wildly in the denominations used for betting. Some simpler home games split chips up such that two or more different chip colors may denote the same value. One friend played in the same home games for years, with red and blue chips always being of equal value, yet insisted on hoarding red chips. He wasn't a particularly good player. No one bothered telling him to focus on his cards and not the color of his chips.

WASHING YOUR HANDS AFTER LOSSES: One avid player insists on washing his hands after losing three big pots in a row, claiming it works every time. This superstition actually makes some sense, as leaving the table, stretching your legs and collecting your thoughts can help prevent you from going on tilt. Try splashing cold water on your face while washing your hands – clears your head. Given the dubious hygiene seen among some players, we're all for periodic washing.

SEPARATING/MIXING UP CHIPS: Some players believe it's bad luck to mix different color chips in their stacks. Others purposely mix them up, sometimes to try and make it difficult for others to survey their holdings while contemplating a bet. You may occasionally see someone keep some chips up their sleeve; that falls less under the category of superstitions and more towards "prepare to get tossed out on your ass."

$50 BILL PHOBIA: Many long-time poker players don't like $50 bills. Though 50s are fairly rare in everyday circulation, the belief holds that you'll find them even less often at a poker table.

WIN A HAND, DO A SHOT: You'll sometimes see a player take a big gulp of his drink or drain a shot after winning a big hand. Those who can handle their liquor can use this tack as a decoy: By pretending they're drunk, they can trap players who change their strategy to try and take advantage of the speech-slurring clown sitting across from them. When Bozo suddenly wipes the smile from his face and lays down the nuts, the loser may start pining for a stiff drink.

> By pretending they're drunk, they can trap players who change their strategy to try and take advantage of the speech-slurring clown sitting across from them.

THE CIRCLE DANCE: A losing streak can be broken, it's said, by standing up and moving around your chair counter-clockwise three times, without turning your back to the table. This has some of the benefits of washing your hands, as you get to step away from the table, stretch your legs and get at least a bit of exercise. It may also be patently insane, but poker players have been called a lot worse. Poker being the highly sedentary game it is, how about 10 jumping jacks and 20 sit-ups to top off the circling?

SOME POKER PLAYER NICKNAMES

PAUL "THE ESKIMO" CLARK

PETER "THE POET" COSTA

JOHNNY "ORIENT EXPRESS" CHAN

ANTONIO "THE MAGICIAN" ESFANDIARI

CHRIS "JESUS" FERGUSON

BRUNO "KING" FITOUSSI

KEN "SKYHAWK" FLATON

GUS "THE GREAT DANE" HANSEN

"ACTION" DAN HARRINGTON

PHIL "POKER BRAT" HELLMUTH

PHIL "UNABOMBER" LAAK

HOWARD "THE PROFESSOR" LEDERER

MARCEL "FLYING DUTCHMAN" LUSKE

RANDY "THE DREAM CRUSHER" JENSEN

PAUL "X-22" MAGRIEL

MIKE "THE MOUTH" MATUSOW

PAUL "DOT COM" PHILLIPS

GREG "FOSSILMAN" RAYMER

SIMON "ACES" TRUMPER

DAVE "THE DEVILFISH" ULLIOTT

RAM "CRAZY HORSE" VASWANI

SOME ODDS AGAINST GETTING DEALT DIFFERENT STARTING HANDS IN SEVEN-CARD STUD

(Odds courtesy of Mike Caro's website, www.poker1.com)

3 aces	5,524 to 1
3 jacks through 3 kings	1,841 to 1
3 sixes through 3 tens	1,104 to 1
3 twos through 3 fives	1,380 to 1
2 aces	75.7 to 1
2 jacks through 2 kings	24.6 to 1
2 sixes through 2 tens	14.3 to 1
2 twos through 2 fives	18.2 to 1
Three parts of a straight flush	85.3 to 1
Three parts of other flush	23.9 to 1
Three parts of other straight	4.76 to 1
ANY three-of-a-kind	424 to 1
ANY pair	4.90 to 1

PHIL GORDON'S MOST COMMON MISTAKES THAT BAD PLAYERS MAKE

- Bad players play too many hands. They don't understand the gap concept.

- Some bad players don't bluff enough.

- Almost all bad players overvalue top pair.

- A lot of bad players underbet the pot.

- In the middle of tournaments, most bad players play too tight.

THE GAP CONCEPT: You should be more willing to raise with a hand than you will be willing to call a raise with a hand. If I'm first to act in middle position with A-10, if I play the pot I'm going to raise it. But if someone raises in front of me, I wouldn't play A-10. There's a very big gap between the hands that you should be willing to raise with and the hands that you should be willing to call a raise with.

UNDERBETTING THE POT: If there's $100 in the pot, maybe you bet $20 making it the right play for the people on the draw to call. You don't bet enough to make the people on the draw pay an appropriate price.

♥ ♦ ♦

POKER GOOD LUCK CHARMS

JOHNNY CHAN'S ORANGE

GREG RAYMER'S FOSSIL

JIM MCMANUS'S PHOTO OF HIS FAMILY

MEN "THE MASTER" NGUYEN'S
BOTTLE OF CORONA

AMIR VAHEDI'S CIGAR

PHIL GORDON'S KEYS TO
NO-LIMIT SUCCESS, PART 3

PLAYING FROM THE BLINDS: When you're in the blinds, you're playing with a negative expectation (even good players will lose a little when out of position) and you just have to overcome that. Playing No-Limit Hold'em out of position is almost always a disaster. Most of the time, you're going to want to give up those blinds much more easily than the average beginner thinks you should. I hardly ever defend my blinds.

If I have a good hand and am out of position, I generally like to reraise and win the pot before the flop. I try to negate the disadvantages of being out of position by putting a lot of chips in before the flop. For instance, if you're all-in in the blind, that negates the positional disadvantage. If you're all-in, it doesn't matter who acts first. Good players will very rarely play out of position if given a choice.

> Just because you flopped top pair doesn't mean you still have to put any more chips in the pot.

The only time that I really consider playing from the blinds is when I have a lot of chips in relation to the size of the blinds and I have a hand that is not likely to be dominated. The other thing that I'd suggest is that if you don't flop a huge hand, you should feel free to get away from it. Just because you flopped top pair doesn't mean you still have to put any more chips in the pot. Good players do their best not to go broke with one pair. One of the best feelings in the world of poker is to flop a set against a guy with one pair. He'll be drawing stone-cold dead.

DOMINATION: Domination is one of the top five principles in No-Limit Hold'em that you have to understand if you want to be a good player. This is it in a nutshell: you're dominated when your opponent has the same high card as you do but you have a lower kicker. Because I don't want to be in a position where I'm dominated, in many instances I'm not as likely to play an A-5 as I am a 6-5. I don't want my opponent who just raised from late position to have

A-Q because then if an ace comes on the flop I'm going to lose a lot of money. A-Q vs. A-10. A-Q vs. K-Q. Those kinds of hands are dominated. In those cases you really only have about a 25% chance to win. However, if you have A-Q and I have 6-7, I've got about a 39% or 40% chance to win. It's almost a coin flip in that situation, but I'm a 3-1 dog when I'm dominated. It's really important that you not play hands that are going to be dominated.

SOME OF MEN "THE MASTER" NGUYEN'S PUPILS

DAVID "DRAGON" PHAM	VAN PHAM
MINH NGUYEN	HAI TRAN

The '80s cemented the idea of newbies rising up to smite the game's heavy hitters, with Stu Ungar leading the charge. Ungar entered the 1980 WSOP Main Event having never played Hold'em before in his life. His total recall and devastating intellect blew away the field, and Ungar won the $385,000 top prize. With bookmakers still giving him long odds the next year, Ungar turned the rare feat of winning back-to-back titles.

It marked another sign to amateurs and newly-minted pros that anyone could win the big prize, and that the cash could change your life forever.

One of the most famous Main Event wins happened in 1982, after Ungar's repeat. One of the last of the old Texas road gamblers, Jack "Treetop" Straus, engineered the most famous World Series of Poker comeback in history. Legend has it that Straus fought his way back from a single $500 chip – which he found under his cigarette pack – to win it all. Though the story's been embellished over time, Straus essentially had enough to cover a couple blinds and little else. After winning a round of blinds, he soon doubled up and was on his way. His miracle comeback sparked his famous line: "If you have a chip and a chair you can win" – later shortened to "A chip and a chair."

With the World Series growing quickly, 1983 proved another pivotal year. When the dust settled, the final two players left at the Main Event were Tom McEvoy and Rod Peate. Unlike the game's elite players – many of whom had become millionaires – McEvoy and Peate were average Joes, middle-limit $10/$20 players with regular jobs who'd won their way into the event via satellites and were now playing for more money than either had seen in his life. With both men strapped financially and $580,000 at stake for the winner (second place would earn a comparatively small $210,000), 1983 marked the first time the event's financial benefit figured to be life-changing for the winner. When McEvoy eventually prevailed, it marked another sign to amateurs and newly-minted pros that anyone could win the big prize, and that the cash could change your life forever.

Though getting on in years, Benny Binion remained the driving force of the Horseshoe and of the WSOP as the mid-'80s rolled in. Looking for a broadcast partner who'd bring the World Series to a wider audience, Binion paid upstart network ESPN $100,000 to produce a show on the WSOP and put it on the air. Though interest was building in the event, the payout was still a must. With the inexperienced, tentative McEvoy and Peate battling in 1983, the event stretched on for days, costing networks thousands as TV crews went deep into overtime.

ESPN's coverage opened the door for the concept of poker celebrities to gain traction. In 1987, top pro Johnny Chan won the $625,000 first prize, gaining his first big measure of attention. His 1988 head-to-head battle with Eric Seidel won him another first-place finish and $700,000 more. His famous slow-play on the final hand became the stuff of legend, instantly cementing Chan's fame and even prompting a later homage in the 1998 poker film *Rounders*. (The next segment on WSOP history starts on page 178.)

TOP POKER HONORS WON
BY AMERICAN ACTORS

BEN AFFLECK'S $356,400 win in the California State Poker Championship at LA's Commerce Casino

TOBEY MAGUIRE'S $95,480 win in a $2,000 buy-in tournament at the Hollywood Park Casino

GABE KAPLAN'S sixth in the World Series of Poker in 1980

♥ ♣ ♦ ♦

DAVID SKLANSKY'S FUNDAMENTAL
THEORY OF POKER

Every time you play a hand differently from the way you would have played it if you could see all your opponents' cards, they gain; and every time you play your hand the same way you would have played it if you could see all their cards, they lose. Conversely, every time opponents play their hands differently from the way they would have if they could see all your cards, they lose; and every time they play their hands the same way they would have played if they could see all your cards, you lose.

WORLD SERIES OF POKER MAIN EVENT
WINNERS AND PRIZE MONEY

YEAR	WINNER	PRIZE MONEY
1970	JOHNNY MOSS	Voted Champion
1971	JOHNNY MOSS	$30,000
1972	AMARILLO SLIM PRESTON	$80,000
1973	PUGGY PEARSON	$130,000
1974	JOHNNY MOSS	$160,000
1975	SAILOR ROBERTS	$210,000
1976	DOYLE BRUNSON	$220,000
1977	DOYLE BRUNSON	$340,000
1978	BOBBY BALDWIN	$210,000
1979	HAL FOWLER	$270,000
1980	STU UNGAR	$385,000
1981	STU UNGAR	$375,000
1982	JACK STRAUS	$520,000
1983	TOM MCEVOY	$580,000
1984	JACK KELLER	$660,000
1985	BILL SMITH	$700,000
1986	BERRY JOHNSTON	$570,000
1987	JOHNNY CHAN	$625,000
1988	JOHNNY CHAN	$700,000
1989	PHIL HELLMUTH	$755,000
1990	MANSOUR MATLOUBI	$895,000
1991	BRAD DAUGHERTY	$1,000,000
1992	HAMID DASTMALCHI	$1,000,000
1993	JIM BECHTEL	$1,000,000
1994	RUSS HAMILTON	$1,000,000
1995	DAN HARRINGTON	$1,000,000
1996	HUCK SEED	$1,000,000
1997	STU UNGAR	$1,000,000
1998	SCOTTY NGUYEN	$1,000,000
1999	NOEL FURLONG	$1,000,000
2000	CHRIS FERGUSON	$1,500,000
2001	CARLOS MORTENSEN	$1,500,000
2002	ROBERT VARKONYI	$2,000,000
2003	CHRIS MONEYMAKER	$2,500,000
2004	GREG RAYMER	$5,000,000

LIST COURTESY OF POKERPAGES.COM

POKER JOKES

(Some jokes courtesy of pokernews.com)

♥ ♣ ♦

THE MILLION DOLLAR DOG

Two dog owners were bragging about the intelligence of their pets.

"The brightest dog I ever had," said one, "was a Great Dane that could play cards. He was a whiz at poker, but I had him put to sleep."

"You had him put to sleep, a bright dog like that? A dog like that would be worth a million dollars."

"Had to," he replied, "Caught him using marked cards!"

♥ ♣ ♦

BLUFFING FOR BEGINNERS

There's a regular game of eight guys playing $3-$6 No-Limit Hold'em. One day a regular brings a friend to come and play. He brings with him a stack of poker books – at the top is *Super System*.

The regulars chuckle and start playing their normal game. Along comes a big pot, heads-up between the newcomer and a regular. The game goes to the river and the regular bets (board is 10-8-J-K-Q, no flush draw). The newbie sits and ponders for a little, then goes all-in. The regular starts contemplating the call, and then the newbie reaches for his drink, knocks over the top book, and reveals *How to Bluff and Win at Poker*. He says "oops" in an honest manner, and restacks the books.

The regular ponders for a few seconds more and calls. The newbie shows the nuts, walks off a hundred bucks richer. He leaves the book on the table. Seeing the book, a regular calls out to him, "Hey man, don't you want your book?" He replies, "No, it looks like you guys need it more than I do."

When he's gone, the regulars open the book and it's empty except for one word on the first page, "Don't."

Told by Doyle Brunson in his book Poker Wisdom of a Champion.

♥ ♣ ♦ ♠

THE END OF THE RAINBOW

A guy was playing $10-$20 Hold'em and was stuck about $300 when he looked down beside the table and saw a little green leprechaun.

"Quit playing poker forever right now and I'll give you a pot of gold worth a million dollars," said the little fellow.

The player shook his head and waved him off. "Let me get even first."

♥ ♣ ♦ ♠

QUESTIONS AND ANSWERS

Q: Do you know what a good poker player eats right before a game?

A: I didn't think you would know.

♥ ♣ ♦ ♠

Q: What do a stage coach driver and a card dealer have in common?

A: Both sit around and look at a bunch of horses' asses all day.

BEST PLACES TO PLAY ONLINE

Eager to play online but not sure where to go? Many poker and even non-poker sites will advertise online cardrooms, claiming theirs is the best place to play your hard-earned cash. Instead of going for the fancy graphic, check out these choices, which include some of the best poker rooms anywhere – online or otherwise. Just make sure to poke around before you fund your account. You don't want to blindly pick a name off a list and start playing without gauging the level of competition, payouts, security and other important factors. In other words: After you're done reading this research, do your own.

⚬ FULL TILT POKER ⚬

WHY TO PLAY? A relatively new site, Full Tilt features big-name poker pros Chris "Jesus" Ferguson, Howard Lederer, Phil Ivey, Erick Lindgren, John Juanda, Eric Seidel, Andy Bloch, Clonie Gowen and Phil Gordon, all playing exclusively there. Playability is solid, with smooth software and graphics. An increasingly popular site, you'll never have a problem finding action, though you may have to wait a long time to play against one of the site's featured stars. Solid customer service, reliable security features and an enticing signup bonus.

⚬ DOYLE'S ROOM ⚬

WHY TO PLAY? Most major poker sites offer bonuses of some kind, and Doyle's Room is among the best in that area. The site allows the player to choose the bonus option that is right for them, ranging from a 25% bonus available for first-time players to an extra 10% bonus offered for those who use online payment system Neteller. You'll have no trouble finding action, and navigation of the room is easy. Backed by poker legend

Doyle Brunson, the site was the only place you could buy Brunson's recently released book *Super System* before the book went to wider release.

♞ POKER STARS ♞

WHY TO PLAY? A massively popular site, Poker Stars has a great look and feel. They've also got some of the best variety of games available anywhere, anytime. The tournament action is particularly strong. If there's an issue with Poker Stars, it's that the competition is generally stronger than at some of the other sites.

♞ POKER CHAMPS ♞

WHY TO PLAY? Gus Hansen's online poker room offers a hard-to-find multi-table view option, which enables you to play up to six tables at once by selecting that option and logging in. One of the best bonus systems around, the Cashflow Program pays as much as $100 a week if you play a couple hours every day at a $5/$10 table. The Cashflow money is earned by playing and accumulating points, with the points converted into cash every Friday. The site's encryption technology ranks among the best in the business.

♞ POKERROOM.COM ♞

WHY TO PLAY? The cut of each pot taken by the host website – also known as the "rake" – doesn't vary much among most major websites. Poker Room does offer a unique feature, though: If you're lucky enough to be playing at a table with four, seven or eight players, you'll pay less of a rake relative to most sites for limits above $1/$2. Having only three games offered (Texas Hold'em, Omaha, Seven-Card Stud) limits your options, though the quality of all three games is good. The site's Java option allows for quick play without daunting downloads.

❧ PARADISE POKER ❧

WHY TO PLAY? One of the longest-running and most popular online poker rooms, the site has been around since 1999. At off-peak times you may find as many as 3,000 players online, 6,000 or more during peak hours. The site offers a wide range of games, including Texas Hold'em, Omaha, Omaha High-Low, Seven-Card Stud and Seven-Card Stud High-Low. The site promises $1,500,000 in a guaranteed prize pool at its Paradise Masters online championship.

❧ ULTIMATE BET ❧

WHY TO PLAY? Backed by Phil Hellmuth, Ultimate Bet features one of the widest assortments of available games anywhere. They include Texas Hold'em, two kinds of Omaha, two kinds of Seven-Card Stud, two kinds of Crazy Pineapple, Double Flop Hold'em, Triple Draw and Kill Games. There's also a wide range of table limits, making it the something-for-everyone destination. Geared towards a global clientele, the site counts 6,000-7,000 players online during peak times.

❧ PARTY POKER ❧

WHY TO PLAY? Fish, plain and simple. Party Poker is an extremely popular site for casual and beginner players and the largest poker room on the Web. That makes it a prime shooting gallery for sharks. A veteran player friend of ours says: "If you want to make money, go to Party Poker." The site tops out at a $30/$60 limit, on the low side among the major poker sites. Bonus points for a slew of payment options.

(Reviews courtesy of pokernews.com and other sources)

HOWARD LEDERER ON WHAT MAKES
A GREAT POKER PLAYER

Howard Lederer is one of the world's great players, known for his professorial bearing at the table and incredible acumen in both cash games and tournaments. Here he talks about where his edge comes from.

That's an impossible question to answer. My edge comes from a lot of places. From my desire to compete, my desire to provide for my family, my desire to be respected by my peers, my natural puzzle-solving mentality. Being a successful poker player is a constantly changing puzzle, a puzzle that becomes more complex as the competition increases and as new games get introduced. It just comes from my desire to do all those things. I can't tell you it's only because I know numbers. There is no one thing that makes you a good poker player. It's really an integration of all the things that go into being a good poker player. So if you're talking about my edge, I do think it's the motivation that gives me the little extra edge. Breaking down what makes a winning poker player is really an impossible task, or at least it's not useful. It's not useful for me to quantify it, to say 30% of my edge comes from my superior knowledge of the math of poker, 55% comes from my steady demeanor and the other 15% comes from my ability to read my opponent – that's not poker. There are as many different ways to win at poker as there are winning poker players. That's one thing I love about the game. I literally believe that.

POKER GAMES WITH FUNNY NAMES

❈ SPIT IN THE OCEAN ❈

How to play: A community-draw game where each
player is dealt four cards and a card is flipped from the
top of the deck. This card is known as the "Spit" card
and is the fifth card in everyone's hand. In a variation
on the game, the dealer may determine that five cards
are dealt to each player, in total giving players six cards
including the Spit card from which each makes their
best five-card hand.

Quick tip: An interesting variation on the game is
Stormy Weather (though some people still call it Spit
in the Ocean). Each player is again dealt four cards
face down. The game then features three community
cards, also dealt face down. After the first betting
round and draw, each community card is flipped over
one at a time, followed each time by a betting round.
At showdown, players make their best five-card hand
with the four cards dealt to them and any *one* of the
three community cards.

❈ HOMAHA ❈

How to play: Each player is dealt four cards face
down, with five cards flipped over in Texas Hold'em
style. You must choose exactly two cards from your
hand to be combined with three of the five community
cards in forming the best possible hand. As the name
implies, the game comes with a twist: No straights are
allowed in the game, and queens are wild.

Quick tip: We're skirting the edges of political correct-
ness here, to be sure. For what it's worth, a gay friend
of ours regularly takes part in this game and finds it to
be a riot, as well as a fun change of pace from stuffy

games of stud or draw. Still, consider your audience. You want people to have fun when they play with you, not to leave offended, never to return.

❤ SCREW YOUR NEIGHBOR ❤

How to play: No ante. Instead, each player puts two piles of chips in front of himself (typical low-stakes games have players put $1 or $2 per pile). Each player is then dealt one card each. Starting left of the dealer, the first player decides if he wants to (a) keep the card or (b) exchange it with the player on his left. Then that player does the same thing, going around the table. A card keeps going around the table until it reaches the dealer. Being last, the dealer can either keep his card or exchange it with the next card from the deck. After that, everybody flips their cards and the player with the lowest card puts one of his piles into the pot.

The game keeps going, but the first person dealt to is now the second player left of the dealer, and the first person left of the dealer becomes the "button." The pattern keeps going that way after each round. Once you lose both of your piles, the game is over for you. The "Screw Your Neighbor" aspect comes from two main premises: First, you're trying to stick the person next to you with the lowest card possible. Second, if a player has an ace in his hand as the card comes around, he flips it over and the player attempting to pass the card around must eat it.

Quick tip: A player may sometimes opt to pass a card on, only to get a lower card in exchange. Watch for a tell in this situation – if you're due to act later, you can often simply opt to keep your 3 or 4, knowing a 2 is sitting in a hand behind you.

10 PLACES TO PLAY POKER ON OR NEAR THE LAS VEGAS STRIP

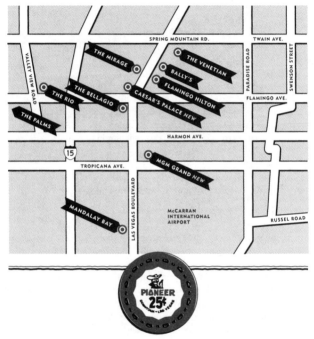

SOME IMAGES SEEN ON POKER CHIPS

CLOWN	HORSE SHOE
JULIUS CAESAR	AIRPLANE
HORSES	BROWN BEAR
CAROUSEL	PARROT
COWBOY BOOT	MISS UNIVERSE
AMERICAN FLAG	KENNY G

THE POKER BOOM

Why is poker bigger than ever before?

One word: television.

Poker had been boiling just beneath the surface of mainstream popular culture for years. Then in March of 2003, it happened. The Travel Channel introduced to America the "hole cam" for its broadcasts of *The World Poker Tour* (the concept of seeing the players' hole cards had been used previously in England on *Late Night Poker*). Because of the hole cam, suddenly it was easy for the viewers at home to see exactly what the players were holding and how they were playing. Every bluff, every tell, every raise, every laydown could be experienced by the audience in a way like never before. Talk about reality television! The same technology was used for the World Series of Poker, broadcast on ESPN later that year. Of course, the tournament was won by Chris Moneymaker, who won his entry to the World Series in a low buy-in online tournament.

> Every bluff, every tell, every raise, every laydown could be experienced by the audience in a way like never before.

Moneymaker's win helped legitimize online poker and made him an instant star. People watching at home learned the game and began to play online, with their friends and in cardrooms. The game's popularity has been on a rising graph ever since.

THE BEST PIECE OF POKER ADVICE EVER GIVEN TO CLONIE GOWEN – OR, WHAT WOULD JESUS DO?

When Clonie Gowen played in her first major tournament, she ended up at the final table heads-up against Humberto Brenes – a legendary Costa Rican pro and the owner of two World Series of Poker bracelets – and suddenly she was intimidated. Despite all her success in poker games around Dallas, this was something a little different. Here's Clonie on what happened next:

I thought "Oh my gosh." At this point I'd played enough poker that I just wasn't intimidated at the table anymore. But it was a different setting, it was a tournament. And Humberto is an excellent player, one of the best in Costa Rica and here I am heads-up with him. My confidence was shot. There was a little break and I asked [World Series of Poker Champion] Chris Ferguson – who is one of the nicest and smartest men in the world – for some advice. I said "Chris, I haven't been in a heads-up situation very often other than in small-stakes games, so what do I do?" He looked very serious and he asked me to step outside with him. I followed him out and he just looks at me and I'm waiting and thinking to myself that he's about to give me something good here and he says, "OK, here it is. Just keep doing what you've been doing."

I ended up getting second place anyway but it still was good advice for me and it's good advice for other players, too. I know I have the skills to play the game if I can find the confidence to do what I need to do. Confidence and positive thinking are just so much a part of anything you do in life.

THE NINE GAMES CURRENTLY PLAYED AT THE WORLD SERIES OF POKER

NO-LIMIT HOLD'EM

LIMIT HOLD'EM

POT-LIMIT HOLD'EM

NO-LIMIT 2 TO 7 DRAW LOWBALL

SEVEN-CARD RAZZ

POT-LIMIT OMAHA

OMAHA HIGH-LOW SPLIT

SEVEN-CARD STUD

SEVEN-CARD STUD HIGH-LOW SPLIT

SOME IMAGES SEEN ON THE FACES OF CARDS

NAKED WOMEN

REPUBLICANS

IRAQI WARLORDS

EVIL FORCES IN EAST SLAVONIC MYTHOLOGY

SHAKESPEARE HEROES AND HEROINES

FIGURES FROM THE TORAH

ANIME CHARACTERS

1932 OLYMPIANS

NAKED WOMEN WITH FARM ANIMALS

CARTOON BEARS

ITALIAN CATS

ALIENS

THE KENNEDYS

PHIL GORDON'S KEYS TO
NO-LIMIT SUCCESS, PART 4

BOARD TEXTURE: When you're analyzing the community cards, a couple of different scenarios are possible. Maybe the board paired or three-suited or there's a flush draw or straight draw out there. What good players do is analyze the board and figure out how many draws their opponent might be on. For instance, if the board comes J-10-9, there are a lot of draws out there for anyone who's playing A-K, A-Q. Someone might have K-Q already. J-10 is a fairly popular hand, so they might have two pair. 8-7 is possible for a straight. If an 8 comes on the turn, then anyone with a queen will have a straight. There are a lot of bad cards that can come on the turn that will make someone a great hand.

Compare that flop to J-7-2 three-suits. There's almost no card that can come that will make someone a straight unless they're playing some wacky hand like 3-5 or something. You're not scared of a 7, you're not scared of a 10. So if you had A-J in that situation, you'd be looking good and you'd want your opponent to be able to play with you because they have very few outs. Board texture is really all about figuring out how much to bet. If I think I have the best hand right now and there are a lot of cards that can come that will scare me, I'm going to

> Board texture is really all about figuring out how much to bet.

bet at least the size of the pot. I want to either win the pot right there or make my opponent pay an appropriate price to draw against me. If there are not a lot of cards that can come to scare me, then I'm only going to bet about half the pot. I want to encourage someone to play. So in that situation where I have A-J and the flop is J-10-9, well, I'm going to bet at least the pot if I decide to bet. I want that person with Q-J or Q-10 or K-J to pay an appropriate price to play further.

> The goal in poker is to try and get your opponent to make the biggest mistake possible.

However, if the flop is J-7-2, I'm only going to bet about half the pot because I want them to bet. I'm not worried about them catching their card on the turn because if they're playing Q-J or J-10, they're only going to hit that card about 6% of the time.

When you only have one pair, you don't have a great hand. So if you're trapping with one pair and trying to check raise, then you're making a mistake. If you check and they check, then they haven't made a mistake. The goal in poker is to try and get your opponent to make the biggest mistake possible. When you have the best hand, you want your opponent to get as many chips into the pot as possible. By doing that, your opponent would be making a mistake. But if they check back at you, they're not making a mistake. When you have the best hand and you slow play, you're not allowing them to make a mistake. You might get them to make a bigger mistake later, but that's a pretty rare circumstance. New players especially very much overdo the slowplaying and they pay for it.

PHIL GORDON ON HOW MUCH TO RAISE BEFORE THE FLOP

 At a full table, if I'm the first person in the pot, I always raise it. I never limp in No-Limit. I think that's just a horrible thing to do. If I'm first to play, I'm going to raise and generally I like to raise about three times the size of the big blind. Sometimes I will vary the size of my raise, not based on my cards but based on my position. I might raise 2.5 from early position, 3-3.5 from middle position and 4 from late. That seems to work better for me.

When I'm raising from early position, I've usually got the nuts. I've got aces or kings or queens or A-K and I'm not really afraid of people playing with me, so I want to encourage them to play. So a raise of 2.5 times the big blind seems about right.

> When I'm raising from early position, I've usually got the nuts.

From middle position, I want to discourage people from playing. I want to raise more to either get heads-up with the blind or to make it difficult for the other players to play, so 3-3.5 seems about right. And from the button I just want to steal the blinds, so 4 works for me.

Likewise, if I'm trying to get cute and I do decide to play 6-5 suited from early position, I'm going to raise also 2.5 times the big blind. I'm still not going to limp. If the play works or if it doesn't work, I still haven't invested a lot of money.

THE PROBLEM WITH LIMPING

The reason I hate limping is that if no one re-raises before the flop, you're not going to give your opponent a chance to define his/her hand clearly. Say you've got aces and the flop comes J-7-2. Well, if the pot wasn't raised preflop, maybe the guy in the blind had 7-2. And when you limp, you're almost always encouraging multi-way action. If you limp, the guy on the button's going to limp, the small blind's going to complete, the big blind's going to see the flop and now you've got four players. And you've got no earthly idea at all what they have.

> If you limp, the guy on the button's going to limp, the small blind's going to complete, the big blind's going to see the flop and now you've got four players. And you've got no earthly idea at all what they have.

Likewise, I always bet my hand if I hit the flop. People know that you're strong if you checkraise. Let's say I've got A-5 and the board comes K-5-5. I'm going to bet out and hope that the guy's got A-K and raises me. People expect you to slowplay, but that's just wrong. Bet out and raise and you're going to get them to commit more chips to the pot.

MARRIED COUPLES WHO BOTH PLAY PROFESSIONAL POKER

Cecelia de Mortensen & Carlos Mortensen

Karina Jett & Chip Jett

Martine Oules & Paul Magriel

MORE POKER JOKES

A POKER EMERGENCY

A doctor answers his phone and hears the familiar voice of a colleague on the other end of the line.

"We need a fourth for poker," said the friend.

"I'll be right over," whispered the doctor.

His wife sees him putting on his coat. "Is it serious?" she asks worriedly.

"Oh yes, quite serious," said the doctor gravely. "In fact, there are three doctors there already!"

A POKER EMERGENCY, PART 2

Six guys were playing poker when Smith loses $500 on a single hand, clutches his chest and drops dead at the table. Showing respect for their fallen comrade, the other five complete their playing time standing up.

Roberts looks around and asks, "Now, who is going to tell the wife?"

They draw straws. Rippington, who is always a loser, picks the short one.

They tell him to be discreet, be gentle, don't make a bad situation any worse than it is.

"Gentlemen! Discreet? I'm the most discreet man you will ever meet. Discretion is my middle name, leave it to me."

Rippington walks over to the Smith house, knocks on the door, the wife answers, asks what he wants.

Rippington says, "Your husband just lost $500 playing cards."

She hollers, "TELL HIM TO DROP DEAD!"

Rippington says, "I'll tell him."

THE DEVIL AND BILL GATES

Bill Gates dies and goes to heaven. Saint Peter greets him at the pearly gates and says, "Bill, you're such a unique individual that we've decided to give you a choice between heaven and hell."

Bill asks if he can get a look at the two options.

Saint Peter says, "Sure, I've got two windows you can look through." He opens the window to heaven and Bill sees lots of angels sitting on clouds plucking harps.

Peter then opens the second window to hell. It's a brightly-lit casino – lots of people drinking, laughing and having a good time. There are naked dancing girls on stage and in the corner a nice little poker room. Doyle, Mike and other poker greats are playing Bill's favorite, $3-$6 Hold'em. There's an empty seat with chips and they wave at Bill to come join them in the game.

Bill tells Saint Peter that he's decided that hell looks like it's more fun and he wants to join the poker game. Saint Peter snaps his fingers and Bill's wish is granted.

Six months go by and Saint Peter decides to see how his friend Bill is doing. He opens the window to hell and there is Bill shackled by his ankles, hanging over a fiery pit. Peter asks him how he likes his new home.

"Saint Peter, this isn't anything like you showed me. What happened?"

"Sorry, Bill, I thought you realized that was just the demo version."

BEST POKER ROOMS IN THE WORLD

The explosion in online poker has shifted much of the game's attention to the Web. But just as the game's marquee event – the World Series of Poker – is played in a brick-and-mortar casino, a wide array of great poker rooms reside in casinos around the country and around the world.

L'AVIATION CLUB DE FRANCE, PARIS, FRANCE

Located in the heart of Paris, l'Aviation Club de France was forged by a group of aviators in 1907. The club is famed for its beautiful décor and upper-crust clientele. The booming popularity of poker and the club's willingness to open its doors wider – the club advertises "the best cash games in Europe" have caused a spike in business – while keeping l'Aviation's charm well intact.

CONCORD CARD CASINO, VIENNA, AUSTRIA

Home of the European World Series of Poker, the casino opened in 1993 as the first 100% privately-owned and financed casino in Austria. The club hosts the usual array of games, including Texas Hold'em, Omaha and various stud games, attracting players from across the continent. While several European governments begin to explore the viability of loosening gambling controls, the Concord remains a prime destination on the largely restricted continent.

CASINO RAY, HELSINKI, FINLAND

The gambling legislation in Finland does not allow private parties to arrange gambling, so Casino RAY is effectively owned by the state, with most of the profits going to various charities. The only casino in Finland, its cardroom lacks the scale of many of the bigger American casinos. Still, in a landscape where many casinos go over the top on garish surroundings, Casino RAY is more subtle, leaving players free to focus on the action at the tables and not blinding gold pillars or other distracting accoutrements. About one-third of the customers are foreign, with another one-third overall being women.

FOXWOODS, MASHANTUCKET, CONNECTICUT

Described by many as more of a city than a casino because of its massive size, Foxwoods is actually six casinos in one, featuring a huge variety of games in its cardrooms, including its poker room. Though you'll find plenty of grinders on their 48th straight hour of play, the resort offers enough four-star accommodations, golf, food and other distractions to keep you from overdosing on $3/$6. The resort rises out of the Connecticut woods, jutting into the sky and towering over anything for miles around. It's a sight to behold, and a favorite among players from all over.

COMMERCE CASINO, CITY OF COMMERCE, CALIFORNIA

The city of Las Vegas built much of its fortune from motorists and vacationers streaming in from Los Angeles – just a four-hour drive away, give or take a few speeding tickets. The city of L.A. long ago realized this trend, erecting such players' havens as the Commerce Casino. As Phil Gordon and Jonathan Grotenstein note in *Poker: The Real Deal*, you'll find a wider variety of poker games here, covering a wider range of limits, than anywhere in the world. "If poker had a heaven," they go on, "it might look something like the Commerce Casino."

HOLLYWOOD PARK CASINO, INGLEWOOD, CALIFORNIA

Is it as classy as l'Aviation? Uh-uh. Does the food compare to Bellagio? Not a chance. But Hollywood Park has a grungy-but-enjoyable vibe going, with the focus on the game at hand. A wide range of games and limits are available; hit the same games a few times and you'll soon make friends (or at least grunting acquaintances) with Hollywood Park's many regulars. You'll find plenty of skilled veterans as well as USC trust-fund babies with dead money here, so choose your tables and your battles carefully.

TAJ MAHAL, ATLANTIC CITY, NEW JERSEY

A favorite among New Yorkers, the Taj gained added fame from Mike McD and Worm's trip there to wipe out the fish and tourists in *Rounders*. The casino hosts Seven-Card Stud, High-Low games, Omaha and of course Hold'Em, with limits ranging from $1-$2 for some Seven-Card games to pot-limit Hold'em. There's even free poker instruction for beginners, according to the Taj's website: "The Taj Mahal Poker Room offers free poker instruction for beginners daily to help you feel comfortable and confident to play by the rules." The lessons learned at the real poker tables get considerably more fun, and often more expensive than "free."

GROSVENOR VICTORIA CASINO, LONDON, ENGLAND

Strict gaming regulations keep options to a minimum in jolly old England, but the Grosvenor does offer six tables for stud poker. Sure, that's a drop in the bucket compared to big-name Vegas casinos, but the action's fast and furious here, the waits long and sometimes equally spirited. The casino hosts The British Open of Poker, one of the game's biggest and most prestigious tournaments.

SOME ONLINE POKER FORUMS

» RGP FORUM
http://www.recpoker.com/groups.php

» TWO PLUS TWO FORUMS
http://forumserver.twoplustwo.com/ubbthreads.php

» FULL CONTACT POKER
http://www.fullcontactpoker.com/poker-forum/

» THE HENDON MOB FORUM
http://www.thehendonmob.com/MobForum/
forum.php?f=1

» POKER HUB
http://pokerhub.com/forums/index.php

» GLOBAL POKER FORUM
http://www.gamma-seven.com/forum/

» POKER ANALYSIS
http://www.pokeranalysis.com/

» POKER-KING.COM
http://www.poker-king.com/poker-king-messages.php

» POKERWORKS.COM
http://pokerworks.pokerclan.com/

» POKERWORDS.COM
http://www.pokerwords.com/forum/

» POKAH!
http://pokah.pokerroom.com/

» HOMEPOKERGAMES.COM
http://www.homepokergames.com/

» KICK ASS POKER
http://www.kickasspoker.com/17forum/

» POKER LINKFARMS:
http://www.poker-www.com/pages/2/
http://dir.yahoo.com/Recreation/Games/
Card_Games/Poker
http://www.pokerlistings.com/
http://www.pokernews.info/

BEST POKER FOODS

The best poker foods must pass several tests. Obviously they should taste good. Most doctors not named Atkins will tell you that brussels sprouts promote better health than a bacon double cheeseburger. That doesn't mean you should eat brussels sprouts at the poker table. Hearty, flavorful fare is a must here.

You also want foods that are easy to make and easy to eat. If poker night equates to guys' night out, you shouldn't expect rack of lamb and crème brûlée. No dish should take more than 20 minutes to prepare and you should be able to eat with your hands.

Perhaps most importantly, poker food can't be excessively messy. If you plan to stop your no-limit freeze-out in mid-stream, kick back and drink merlot for an hour, fine. But most Friday night games don't swing that way. With that in mind, you generally want to avoid foods that make your friends' fingers sticky or slimy. Foods such as spare ribs and fried chicken are only recommended if everyone's willing to invest enough time scrubbing the sauce and grease off their hands, lest they mess up your cards or your brand spankin' new poker table.

An easier route would be choosing one of the following dishes: ▶▶

❄ BIG SLICK BRUSCHETTA ❄

Sure, it has a fancy name. But bruschetta's basically big hunks of bread with lots of good stuff thrown on top. Go the extra mile if you can for ingredients, as the right bread and right tomatoes will make a difference while still keeping the overall cost of making the dish reasonable. Serves eight.

❱❱ INGREDIENTS

12 to 14 fresh ripe plum tomatoes (1½ to 2 pounds)

2 tablespoons minced garlic

2 tablespoons minced shallots

1 cup fresh basil leaves

1 teaspoon fresh lemon juice

Salt and coarsely ground black pepper, to taste

⅓ cup plus another ¼ cup extra virgin olive oil

3 cloves garlic, slivered

8 thick slices round peasant bread

❱❱ INSTRUCTIONS

1. *Cut the tomatoes into ¼-inch dice and place in a bowl. Toss with the minced garlic and shallots.*

2. *Chop the basil coarsely and add to the tomatoes, along with the lemon juice, salt and pepper, and ⅓ cup olive oil. Set aside.*

3. *Heat the ¼-cup olive oil in a small skillet. Sauté the slivered garlic until golden, two to three minutes. Discard the garlic and reserve the oil.*

4. *Toast the bread and cut each slice in half. Arrange the slices on eight small plates. Brush the garlic-flavored oil over each slice, spoon the tomato mixture over the bread and serve immediately. The mixture should be at room temperature.*

✹ CHECK RAISIN' CAJUN POPCORN SHRIMP ✹

If you don't plan to stop for a true sit-down meal, this disk provides some substance for a quick-bite food. Makes hors d'oeuvres for eight – increase quantities accordingly for a bigger group.

▶▶ INGREDIENTS

1 pound large shrimp

1 cup unbleached all-purpose flour

1 tablespoon cayenne pepper

1 tablespoon chili powder

1 tablespoon ground cumin

1 teaspoon freshly ground black pepper

½ teaspoon salt

1 cup corn oil

Tabasco sauce, to taste

▶▶ INSTRUCTIONS

1. *Peel and devein the shrimp. Cut them into ½-inch pieces.*

2. *Combine the flour, cayenne, chili powder, cumin, black pepper and salt in medium-size bowl.*

3. *Heat the oil in a large skillet. Dredge the shrimp in the flour mixture, shaking off any excess. Fry them quickly over high heat until brown and crisp, occasionally adding a dash of Tabasco for spice. Drain on paper towels.*

To serve, spear each piece with a toothpick to prevent greasy poker fingers.

❧ SEVEN (CARD STUD) LAYER DIP ❧

This is perfect for poker night because it's easy to make, filling and you don't have to get up from the table to eat it. The Earl of Sandwich would be proud.

❱❱ INGREDIENTS

2 cans refried beans

1 can (4 ounces) green chiles, drained

1 envelope of taco seasoning mix

2 ripe avocados, peeled and pitted

1 tablespoon lemon juice

1 jar taco sauce or 2 large tomatoes, chopped

1½ cups sour cream

3 cups shredded lettuce

1½ cups (6 ounces) shredded cheese

1 small can sliced ripe olives

tortilla chips

❱❱ INSTRUCTIONS

1. *In a medium bowl, mix together refried beans, green chiles and taco seasoning mix. Spread on a 12-inch round platter or large casserole dish.*

2. *Blend avocados, lemon juice, and ½ cup taco sauce until smooth. Spread on top of bean mixture. Spread sour cream on top of avocado mixture. Top with shredded lettuce, cheese, taco sauce (or chopped tomatoes) and olive slices.*

3. *Serve with chips.*

It guarantees a full house.

SOME COOL POKER SOFTWARE

TURBO POKER: Wilson's Turbo Poker Series is the clear market leader for poker software. An excellent teaching tool for beginners, the software is particularly great for practicing general strategies and getting a feel for the game. There are many stories of inexperienced tournament players placing high after a few months of practice with Turbo Texas Hold'em ($89.95) and Tournament Turbo Texas Hold'em ($59.95), including Jim McManus, the author of *Positively Fifth Street*. Among the game's endorsers is the Mad Genius of Poker himself, Mike Caro. The games in Wilson's Turbo Poker series aren't cheap, but there are downloadable demos of each game so you can see what you're getting. Another advantage of the Turbo line is that they offer programs for a full range of games, including Seven-Card Stud, Seven-Stud 8 or Better, Omaha High, and Omaha High-Low Split. ➥ *http://wilsonsoftware.com/*

POKER ACADEMY: Poker Academy's reasonably priced standard version ($39) is an excellent value buy for beginners. And in terms of Hold'em, the Poker Academy standard edition already gives the Turbo Series a run for its money. One reason Poker Academy is such an effective training tool is that the game adjusts and advances as you do, providing escalating challenges that test your strategies. For the more serious player, the Poker Academy Pro version ($129) is what you want. Like the standard edition, it uses some of the world's most advanced artificial intelligence technology to help you improve your game. But in Poker Academy Pro, the bots are hyper-adaptive, punishing opponents who lose their focus. Playing against them is a great way to advance your game to the next level. The company's ambition is to turn

Poker Academy Pro into the poker version of IBM's Deep Blue. ➤ *http://www.poki-poker.com*

ACESPADE: Acespade offers an array of poker simulation software that has been praised by the likes of noted poker gurus David Sklansky and Mason Malmuth. ➤ *http://www.acespade-software.com/*

IPOKER: This Macintosh-only game contains 101 different versions of poker and allows you to customize your own games as well. $29.99. ➤ *http://www.ouzts.net/iPoker/*

DAVE O'BRIEN'S SMOKE'EM POKER: A poker simulation game that's free? Absolutely. Download at: ➤ *http://www.free-games-net.com/games/sempoker.shtml*

✦ ✦ ✦ ✦

SOME THOUGHTS ON PHIL IVEY'S NICKNAME

Phil Ivey is one of the most exciting players in the world to watch. His three bracelets at the 2002 World Series of Poker equaled a record. And he's even more of a cash game threat than he is a tournament player. You see a lot of places where Phil Ivey is called "The Tiger Woods of Poker." His youth, charisma and phenomenal skill explain the nickname but Phil understandably downplays it, saying "Tiger Woods is the best in his game. I'm not there yet." A dealer at Harrah's in Atlantic City mentioned another nickname of Ivey's. Apparently when Phil was underage, he still used to play in the Atlantic City casinos using a fake ID. The name of the guy on the ID was Jerome. Apparently even now, when Ivey plays in certain casinos, there are still some people who call him Jerome.

ROBERT WILLIAMSON III ON
WHAT HE LIKES BETTER ABOUT CASH
GAMES OVER TOURNAMENTS

At this point in my life, I'm about 50/50 in terms of preference of cash games and tournaments, but for most of my life, there's no question that I preferred cash games. By far. I like the consistency. There are not the swings that the tournaments have. In tournaments, you could play your best for one solid year and never win a tournament. In cash games, if you play your best for one solid year and never win, you better quit playing poker. In other words, the sample size doesn't need to be near as great for the true cream to rise to the top. If I can't beat a money game within a month, chances are I'm not going to beat it. Either I'm getting hustled, cheated or I'm not as good at that game as I thought I was.

Also, I like being able to control the factors the way you can in a cash game. In a tournament, you get told, here's the rules, here's the buy-in, here's the pay-out. In a cash game, at the high limits, we negotiate the games we're going to play, we negotiate how high we're going to play. There's even a negotiation involved for how long we're going to play usually. And I get to pick my exact opponents? That's a no-brainer.

♥ ♦ ♦ ♦

PHIL GORDON ON WHY HE PREFERS
TOURNAMENTS OVER CASH GAMES

It doesn't take much to take your A game to your D game. Sometimes players are on tilt, maybe they've played too many hours. I don't play a lot of cash games. I try to play a limited schedule. I try to look at poker the way that Tiger Woods looks at golf. He prepares for the majors. He gets up for the big events and that enables him to play better. I don't understand how people play 350 tournaments a year like some of these guys do. I would kill myself. I understand why certain players prefer cash games. The great thing about tournaments for me is that they require a constantly changing strategy. I don't like cash games because every hand that you play is just like every other hand. You're never short-stacked, you're never on the bubble, you're never big-stacked. Each situation is different, whereas cash games are just a grind, one bet at a time.

A FEW THINGS THAT ROBERT WILLIAMSON III HAS BET ON

Foosball

Air Hockey

Pitching Quarters (Despite being one of the world's great quarter pitchers, he once notably lost a match to Marlon Santos, the best quarter pitcher in the world.)

Intra-Game Football Must-Bets (Will Tom Brady throw for 100 yards this half? Which team will score more in the next eight minutes? Etc. With a must-bet, if you ask for a line, you have to take one side or the other.)

Could his team beat the team led by Todd Brunson (Doyle's son) at four person volleyball? (He lost, but one of his teammates was on the take.)

Could he swim across a bay in San Diego? (Cancelled due to shark infested waters.)

Could he swim across a silt-filled pond in a certain amount of time? (He could.)

Would he stay in a shallow tank with stingrays for 60 seconds? (He didn't know about the stingrays, but he did.)

Could he kick an inflatable ball onto a roof? (Eventually, he did.)

NON-POKER POKER GAMES

Variety is supposedly the spice of life – it can definitely spice up your weekly poker game. Here are a few non-poker games you can mix into your poker night.

BLACKJACK: *How to play:* Make sure everyone at the table gets a chance to be dealer, as the house always holds a small edge. Set a time limit for the game so it remains a light, change-of-pace game and not a huge monkey wrench in your poker night.

➧ *Quick tip:* Odds are you know the basics of black-jack. You want to take advantage of every opportunity as aggressively as you can. Got nine against a five? Double down immediately. Look for split opportunities that bring good odds and play them hard. A healthy dose of luck combined with some smart play can inflate your bankroll and let you play more big pots later in the night when you're ready to go back to poker.

7-27: *How to play:* Ante up, then deal each player one card face down and one up. The object is to get closest to 7 or 27 or both, though it's almost always a split-pot game. A=1 or 11, 2=2, 3=3, etc....10=10, face cards=½ a point. Bets start after you get your cards, and then players have the option of taking a card. You can pass once, but if you pass in two consecutive rounds, you are locked and can never hit again. After each dealing round, players bet. If no one takes a card in a round, there are no bets. If that happens twice in a row, the dealing ends and final bets are made before players pick whether to go high, low or pig (A-A-5 is 7 and 27, auto-matic winner for both). For split pots, the player closest to 7 takes half, and the other half goes to the player who had closest to 27. Note that 6½ beats 7½, and 27½ beats 26½. If there is a tie, then most cards to 7 (or whatever the winning low hand was) wins and least cards to 27 (or whatever the winning high hand was) wins.

➥ *Quick tip:* There are major bluffing possibilities in this game, especially if you have 6 showing with your face-down card. Bet your hand hard and you may convince all other players to try and win with closest to 27. That makes you an automatic winner going low, unless a player pulls the rare A-A-5. Conversely, if you see a player with 6 or 7 showing betting hard and you can't make a low hand, consider folding right away.

ACEY DEUCEY: *How to play:* A simple game of chance – with card-counting a helpful tool – the dealer starts the game by flipping over two cards face up for one player at a time to play. Each player then places a bet based on the odds of the third card to be flipped falling between the first two cards. Thus, if K-2 is flipped, you want to bet heavily, usually the entire pot (if you're first to act, that would consist of the initial round of antes). If an ace is the first card flipped over, the player must designate it high or low before seeing the second card – making card-counting all the more important. An ace flipped on the second card is automatically high. Minimum bets should be required even when no winning hand is possible.

➥ *Quick tip:* When your game has progressed to Acey Deucey time, you may as well let it all hang out. In addition to minimum bets, enforce stiff penalties for "goal-posting." In other words, if you bet $10 in the K-2 example above and the third card is a K, the player should be required to pay double his bet. A few goalposts on big bets and suddenly you've got a pot that will change the outcome of the final winner's night – maybe his month.

BUYING THE RIGHT POKER EQUIPMENT: THE RIGHT STUFF

When you're ready to buy your own chips and/or a table, make sure you do your homework. Put quality first. Look for equipment with an eye towards the longterm. If you can't afford something you desire now, keep saving. Don't settle for less and have to replace what you buy in a few months anyway.

Educate yourself and your due diligence will be rewarded. Click and buy on impulse the first chip set you see online and you'll be sorry.

CHIPS: If the price is too good to be true, proceed cautiously. The materials used to manufacture chips vary greatly and quality control is not the primary concern of the overseas factories that manufacture the cheap stuff. They may resemble the real thing, but that's all. Chips come in a variety of weights, materials and designs in a range of prices, so decide what is appropriate for your level of play. If you're a recreational player who will never play for more than $20 a night, then maybe those plastic chips are OK for you.

> If the price is too good to be true, proceed cautiously.

On the other hand, if you take the game seriously, we recommend taking a step up. True clay chips are no longer manufactured, but "clay composites" are an excellent facsimile. They feel good in your hands and make chip tricks easier. Look for clay composite chips that weigh 11.5 grams or 13.5 grams – anything less and you won't be happy. For more information about poker chips, check out:
http://www.mynameismatt.com/cg/

TABLES: Of course, one doesn't need to purchase a poker table to play poker – in a pinch, any kitchen table will do. But you'll be impressed with how much your game play will improve on an actual table. At the very least, you should consider buying a tabletop that can be unfolded over another table to provide an instant poker room vibe. Cards move better and have less chance of being exposed in transit across felt. Chips may be tossed into the pot much more easily on a soft felt surface that will effectively hold, or catch, them. The hard, uncovered surfaces of everyday tables encourage chips to roll away, add unnecessary clatter and can even leave permanent marks.

In general, there are three categories of table: tabletop overlays, folding leg tables and pedestal or fixed-leg tables. Budget and space constraints will dictate which table is best for your game. Prices range from $20 fold-out tabletops with faux-felt (on e-Bay) to $6,000 cardroom-quality tables that come with a lifetime guarantee, brass and chrome base finishes, foot rails, padded arm rests and a 3/8" foam cushion under the playing surface. With a host of options to choose from, there is no reason why you can't find the right table for your home game. Remember, if you build it, they will come.

BUYING THE RIGHT PLAYING CARDS

PLAYING CARDS: Standard playing cards are 3.5" long. Poker-size (wide) cards are 2.5" (62mm) wide and bridge-size cards are 2.25" (57mm) wide. Most casinos and poker rooms use bridge-size cards because they are easier to handle and shuffle.

There are two types of playing cards: plastic-coated and plastic. Plastic-coated cards are paper cards that have been coated in plastic. They are not as durable as 100% plastic cards. Plastic-coated cards are the most widely available (Bicycle, Bee, Aviator, etc.) and may be purchased for a few dollars per deck. If using these, buy them in bulk from wholesale retailers and you'll be glad that you had such foresight later.

> If you're hosting a home game, you should provide new decks for each occasion.

If you're hosting a home game, you should provide new decks for each occasion – most games employ two decks simultaneously to keep the action moving while one deck is being shuffled. Leave the unopened decks on the table prior to play. This demonstrates that the cards (presumably) have not been marked, or tampered with, and that a fair game is at hand.

Good playing cards make a difference and plastic playing cards are more durable than paper cards. They resist creases, rips, markings and tears. They last longer, can be shuffled easier and slide across the table better thanks to the smooth finish. Spill some beer? Wipe plastic cards with a damp cloth and play on. Plastic card manufactures like KEM Cards, Royal, A Plus Cards, COPAG, Gemaco, Dal Negro and others charge anywhere from $4 to $13 per deck.

ODDS OF CERTAIN OCCURRENCES IN HOLD'EM

(Odds courtesy of Mike Caro's website, http://www.poker1.com)

Holding a pair before the flop 5.88%

Holding two suited cards before the flop 23.53%

Getting dealt A-A or K-K 0.9%

Getting dealt A-K 1.21%

Getting dealt at least one ace 14.93%

If you hold a pair, you'll see at least one more of that card on the flop 11.76%

You'll pair one of your unpaired hole cards on the flop 32.43%

If you hold two suited cards, you'll flop at least a four flush 11.79%

If you have a four flush after the flop, you'll make it 34.97%

If you have four cards of an open-ended straight flush 8.42%

If you have four cards of an open-ended straight flush, you'll make at least a straight 54.12%

If you have two pair after the flop, you will make a full house or better 16.74%

If you have three-of-a-kind after the flop, you will make a full house or better 33.4%

If you have a pair after the flop, you'll end up with trips or quads 8.42%

STRIP POKER

$100

$80

$60

$20

ALL-IN

PHIL HELLMUTH, JR., ON GUESSING YOUR OPPONENT'S EXACT TWO HOLE CARDS

Obviously, the ability to put your opponent on a hand is essential to success in poker, in particular in No-Limit Hold'em. I try to take this idea to the next level by incorporating a little game when I play No-Limit Hold'em. I try to guess the exact two cards my opponent has. I'll even venture a guess out loud when I feel confident about it. How do I do it? The keys are practice, logic and deductive reasoning. By the time someone has acted on his hand three times, a lot of additional information has become available.

I ask myself the following questions:

1. How much did he bet each time?
2. What did it seem he wanted his opponents to do each time?
3. Was he acting weak or strong?
4. How weak or how strong?
5. What did he have the last time he acted this way?
6. Did it seem like he was acting at all?

I have a very good poker memory and asking myself these questions, along with assessing my opponent's reactions to what is happening on the board, allow me to narrow his hand down to a few choices, perhaps a pair of tens, jacks or queens. Then I refine my guess based on what I remember about how my opponent had acted in situations in the past. This guessing game isn't easy and it takes a lot of practice to get good at it. But don't get discouraged if you have trouble doing it at first. If you keep at it, your reads will get better and better and this will help your game immeasurably in the long run.

SOME GREAT FEMALE PLAYERS

Apologies for even calling these women "great female" players. The fact is that they're just great players all-around. In no particular order:

ANNIE DUKE: This mother of four is truly one of the game's elite players. Taught the game by her brother, Howard Lederer, Annie's career has featured many major tournament wins and an amazing 24 in-the-money finishes in various events at the World Series of Poker. In 2004 she had a career year, counting among her wins three important tournaments playing three different games. She won her first WSOP bracelet in the Omaha High-Low event, she won the $2,500 Limit Hold'em at the Bellagio, and she won ESPN's $2 million Tournament of Champions.

JENNIFER HARMAN: It's a testament to what a great player Jennifer Harman is that she's mainly a cash game player and yet she owns two WSOP bracelets. An expert at a variety of games, she contributed the Limit Hold'em chapter to Doyle Brunson's new book, *SuperSystem 2*. On the cash game front, she plays regularly in some of the biggest side games in the world. She's quoted in Ron Rose's book *Poker Aces* as saying, "I enjoy the challenge of playing with the best. It's a constant learning experience. I make mistakes, but as long as I learn something from those mistakes, they can actually be good for me."

LUCY ROKACH: The preeminent female player in Europe, this former teacher and car dealer's tournament wins include firsts at the 2004 British Open Limit Hold'em event, the 2001 Aviation Club Winter Tournament No Limit Hold'em Championship and two wins (2001 and 2003) at the Irish Winter Tournament No-Limit Hold'em Championship. She was also a recipient of a Lifetime Achievement Award at the 2003 European Poker Awards.

KATHY LIEBERT: Kathy Liebert's been playing poker seriously since 1991 and has a number of big tournament wins to her credit, including first place in the Party Poker Million No-Limit Hold'em Championship in 2002, where she became the first woman to ever win a $1 million tournament. She won her first World Series bracelet in 2004 in the Limit Hold'em Shootout.

CLONIE GOWEN: Clonie's another known primarily for her cash game prowess, but this former Miss Teen Oklahoma has been on an impressive tournament run as well. She earned a top-ten finish at the World Poker Tour Costa Rica Classic and won the inaugural WPT Ladies' Night Challenge.

BARBARA ENRIGHT: Barbara Enright was the first woman to have reached the final table at the World Series of Poker, having finished fifth in 1995. She first played poker at age four and has been busting out opponents ever since. She owns three WSOP bracelets (two for the Ladies' Event and one for Pot-Limit Hold'em).

KATHY LIEBERT'S TOP 12
MOMENTS FOR WOMEN IN POKER

⚜ 1982 ⚜

Vera Richmond is the first woman to win an open event at the World Series of Poker (ace to five draw)

⚜ 1995 ⚜

Barbara Enright becomes the first woman to make the final table at the World Series of Poker Main Event, finishing fifth.

⚜ 1996 ⚜

Barbara Enright wins the Pot-Limit Hold'em at the WSOP.

⚜ 1997 ⚜

Linda Johnson wins a World Series Open (Razz).

⚜ 2000 ⚜

Jennifer Harman wins the $5,000 Deuce-to-Seven, No-Limit Lowball Championship at the WSOP after a few minutes of coaching from Howard Lederer in a game she'd never played before.

⚜ 2002 ⚜

Jennifer Harman dominates the final table of the $5,000 Limit Hold'em event at the WSOP, taking home $212,440 and her second WSOP gold bracelet – marking the first time a woman had won two WSOP open titles.

❈ 2002 ❈

Kathy Liebert wins the first PartyPoker.com Million, becoming the first woman to win a major international tournament and the first to capture a $1 million first prize.

❈ 2003 ❈

The World Poker Tour hosts the first Ladies' Night show on the Travel Channel. Six of the top women in the game participate – Kathy Liebert, Annie Duke, Jennifer Harman, Maureen Feduniak and newcomers Clonie Gowen and Evelyn Ng. Gowen upsets the favorites to be crowned first Ladies' Night Champion.

❈ 2004 ❈

Jennifer Harman claims the largest pot in history in a "cash" game at a major casino, $1.7 million, at the Bellagio.

❈ 2004 ❈

Three women win World Series of Poker events in one year – Kathy Liebert ($110,140/$1,500 Limit Hold'em), Annie Duke ($137,860/$2,000 Omaha High-Low) and Cindy Violette ($135,900/Seven Card Stud High/Low).

❈ 2004 ❈

Annie Duke wins the World Series of Poker Tournament of Champions for a $2 million payday. Among the top players she beats are her brother Howard Lederer, Phil Hellmuth, Phil Ivey, Chip Reese, Doyle Brunson, TJ Cloutier, Greg Raymer, Johnny Chan and Daniel Negreanu.

❈ 2005 ❈

Kathy Liebert wins GSN's *PokerRoyale: Battle of the Sexes* against six men and her five female teammates.

Johnny Chan nearly won his third title in a row in 1989, but he had to settle for second place. Instead, Phil Hellmuth fought through the pack to become the youngest-ever winner of the Main Event. With his loud, boisterous antics at the table, he drove opposing players to distraction while proving a natural for the TV cameras. With Chan and Hellmuth stoking the fire, the Main Event grew to more than 200 players. "Suddenly it was a much bigger event," Grotenstein said.

> With his loud, boisterous antics at the table, he drove opposing players to distraction.

So much bigger that 1991 marked the first year that top prize reached $1 million, with Brad Daugherty nabbing the honor. Though the 1990s saw steady growth, much of the backstory present in the '70s and '80s faded. In 1994 the Horseshoe offered the Main Event winner his weight in silver in addition to the $1 million grand prize. When Russ Hamilton – easily the biggest guy at the table – won the prize, the Binions (Benny had died in 1989) were out a few thousand more than they expected. "Action" Dan Harrington, so nicknamed as an ironic statement on his tight play, won the Main Event in 1995, the first player to come out of New York City's famous Mayfair Poker Club to win the WSOP. Harrington, fellow Mayfair alum Howard Lederer and others would emerge as the game's new elite, parlaying cerebral approaches to the game into big winnings.

As the '90s wound down, the World Series became a series of contrasts. Though the event was growing, further aided by the success of *Rounders* and other forms of publicity, a family feud thrust the event, as well as the Horseshoe, into jeopardy. After Benny Binion's widow died in 1993, his children began fighting over control of the Horseshoe. The oldest son, Jack Binion, had helped run the casino since the 1960s and was given most of the initial responsibilities after his father's death. But his sister Becky soon fought back, accusing Jack of mismanagement. A nasty court battle ensued, stretching from 1996 all the way to 1999. Another brother, Ted Binion, lost his gaming license and was ordered to sell his share due to drug problems and other issues. When Jack didn't have enough money to buy all of Ted's stake, Becky bought it instead. That led to Ted taking over the Binions' riverboat gambling business, with Becky assuming control of the Horseshoe and the WSOP. (The final segment on WSOP history starts on page 188.)

(The final segment on WSOP history starts on page 188.)

♥ ♣ ♦ ♠

MORE POKER ON TV

M*A*S*H: If there's any show that can challenge *The Odd Couple*'s title as poker's greatest sitcom, it's this classic medical/war satire. Hawkeye and Trapper John (and later, that wussy B.J.) always had a good game going around their still. Where else could you win a pair of long johns during a Korean winter with a full house?

THE BERNIE MAC SHOW: Comedian Bernie Mac's sitcom carries on the tradition of shows like *The Odd Couple* and later *Roseanne* by occasionally letting us sit in on Bernie's regular game with his regular crew. There's not a lot of cards or card-playing discussed, but home poker game is a great way to get a roomful of characters to voice their opinions on that episode's issues in one scene.

BEST WEIRD, REGIONAL OR NOT-AS-WIDELY KNOWN HOME GAMES

You've seen the traditional casino games. For you and your night poker buddies, that's not enough. Every home game from Mississippi to Montreal inevitably includes some games native to your part of the world. If you're looking for new additions to your own home game, consider these funky alternatives:

✦ MAGIC 10s ✦

How to play: A split-pot game. Everybody antes, then five cards are dealt. The object is to get the highest or lowest (or both) *point* totals, using the following system: A=1 or 11, 2=2, 3=3, etc....10=0 or 10, face cards=10. After a round of betting, five cards are flipped face up from the deck (with a round of betting after each flip). If you have any of the face-up cards in your hand, you must discard them and show them to the other players.

After all the cards are flipped and all betting is done, each player decides whether to go high, low or "pig," with the highest and lowest usually splitting the pot. The rare case to go pig might be on a hand like this: A-A-10-10-10 (2 points *and* 52 points). To win, the player going pig must win both outright, no ties allowed. The other way to win all of the pot is if while the face-up cards are being shown, you have all of those cards and you drop your whole hand before the high/low decision even happens. At that point the game ends early.

Quick tip: A game of extremes, it's a good idea to fold early and save your money if you're dealt more than one middle card – often just one 6 or 7 is enough to warrant a fold.

Magic 10 variation: "48", which features four cards dealt to each player, eight pulled face-up from the deck, betting between each round (cards have same values as Magic 10s).

✖ 3-5-7 ✖

How to play: Everyone gets three cards, 3s are wild. Everyone antes. Starting from left of the dealer, each player must decide whether to match the pot or fold based on the strength of his hand (no flushes or straights allowed, three-of-a-kind is the best hand). The players left in the hand then all look at each others' cards. The player with the best hand takes what's in the pot; the losers must each match what's in the pot.

In round two, the dealer deals two more cards, with everyone now holding five cards total (the players who folded in round one are allowed back in). Here best poker hand using regular rules wins, with 5s wild. Same betting and payout rules apply. Third round is the same, only each player now gets seven cards, 7s are wild. The game ends when only one person stays in, which can occur after any round.

✖ AUCTION ✖

How to play: Ante up, then each person is dealt a five-card poker hand. Five cards are then placed in a row face down. The first card is flipped over, and the card is auctioned off to the highest bidder. That bidder then takes that card and replaces it with one from his hand, face down. The second card is then flipped over and bid on, and so on, with betting occurring after every round. If no one bids on a card, it remains face up and dead, and the game ends after five cards are face up. A round of final betting then occurs, after which the players left reveal their hands.

JOHN VORHAUS ON HOW TO SET UP
A NO-LIMIT HOLD'EM TOURNAMENT
FOR YOUR HOME GAME

Home game tournaments are a great innovation. They give people what they want by satisfying the poker buzz and they give a chance to learn how to play no-limit poker without risking too much bankroll.

TIMING: The appropriate time to do a home game tournament is at the end of an evening. If you run at the start of the night, when people bust out they have to sit there twiddling their thumbs waiting for the tournament to end. But if you bust out at the end of the night you have the choice of sticking around to kibbitz or going home.

> If you bust out at the end of the night you have the choice of sticking around to kibbitz or going home.

BUY-IN: Choose your buy-in by consensus. Often the home game tournament buy-in will be about one-half of the cash game buy-in. If your players usually start out with $100, the tournament buy-in might be $50. If a player busts out early, he or she won't feel so badly about it if the buy-in is reduced, and there will still be enough money in the pool to ensure you are playing for a sizable pot.

CHIPS: For a one table tournament where your buy-in is less than $100, it's still not a bad idea to give out denominations of the equivalent of $100 in chips anyway (100 tournament chips). This will ensure that the players get the right amount of play for their chips and will make setting the blinds easier.

THE CLOCK: You need to set the intervals at which the blinds and limits will increase. Moving them up every 15 or 20 minutes is standard.

BLINDS: You need to agree on what your blind structure is going to be. If your players are starting with $100 in chips, you might do something like this:

LEVEL	BLINDS	
1	$1	$1.50
2	$1.50	$2.50
3	$2.50	$5
4	$5	$10
5	$10	$20
6	$20	$40

PAYOUT: Typically, payout for a home game tournament will be 50% to the winner, 30% to second place and 20% to third place, but you can adjust this as you see fit.

DISPUTES: The host doubles as the tournament director – if disputes arise, you've got to adjudicate those disputes. Again, if you can't be right, be loud.

For additional information on home tournaments and more, check out http://www.homepokertourney.com.

AMARILLO SLIM'S TOP TEN
KEYS TO POKER SUCCESS

1. Play the players more than you play the cards.

2. Choose the right opponents. If you don't see a sucker at the table, you're it.

3. Never play with money you can't afford to lose.

4. Be tight and aggressive; don't play many hands, but when you do, be prepared to move in.

5. Always be observing at a poker game. The minute you're there, you're working.

6. Watch the other players for tells before you look at your own cards.

7. Diversify your play so other players can't pick up tells on you.

8. Choose your speed based on the direction of the game. Play slow in a fast game and fast in a slow game.

9. Be able to quit a loser, and for goodness sake, keep playing when you're winning.

10. Conduct yourself honorably so you're always invited back.

JOHN VORHAUS' HOUSE RULES

BUY-IN Your $100 gets you $90 in chips, food and drink

BETTING LIMITS $1 and $2 at any time; $4 for the last round of betting.

THREE RAISE LIMIT One bet and three raises are allowed during each betting round. Check raising is allowed (see pg. 95).

TYPES OF GAMES It's dealer's choice but no wild cards are allowed.

BEST LOW Wheel low is best low.

EIGHT MUST Unless otherwise stated by the dealer, in all high-low splits the low must qualify (see pg. 95).

CHIP DECLARE All players declare simultaneously. One chip in hand is low. Two chips in hand is high. Three chips in hand is both (pig). No bet after the declare.

PIG RULE If you try to win both low and high, you must win both sides outright to win the pot. A tie is the same as a loss.

BACK-IN RULE If a player goes pig and is eliminated, the remaining players with the best high and best low split the pot, regardless of whom the pig might have beaten.

GOING LIGHT Going light is allowed, but the player must make up his lights immediately upon completion of the hand.

TIE HANDS Tie hands split the pot; the extra chip, if any, goes to the player closest to the dealer's left.

ANTES The dealer antes for the table.

MISDEALS Second exposed card equals misdeal; incorrect hands can only be corrected before any action has been taken.

CREDIT No credit extended; no exceptions.

THE HOUSE RULES Decision of the house is final; no whinging.

POKER PROFILE: STU UNGAR

Stu Ungar may well have been the greatest card player who ever lived. Born in New York City in 1953, Stu "The Kid" Ungar won his first gin rummy tournament at the age of 10. Combining his unnaturally high IQ with a photographic memory, Ungar leveraged his unique prowess at cards from then on, dropping out of school to hustle some of New York's top gin rummy players. He routinely won thousands of dollars from players four or five times his age. Unfortunately, he could as easily lose $10,000 in a few days at the Belmont and Aqueduct horse tracks.

Ungar was so good at gin rummy that he was quickly running out of opponents willing to play against him, so he turned his sights to other games. He went to Las Vegas shortly after his 21st birthday but before he even checked into his hotel he lost his entire $30,000 stake playing table games. As good as he was at cards, he couldn't get his sports betting under control and he amassed large debts back in New York.

Ungar moved to Las Vegas in 1978. Plying his gin rummy skills and counting cards at blackjack enabled him to wipe clean past debts, but pit bosses soon banned him and his action all but dried up again.

Then Ungar learned how to play Texas Hold'em. In 1980, Ungar entered the World Series of Poker. The bold, fearless 27-year-old shocked the poker world by winning the $365,000 tournament over the game's best players. At the time, he was the youngest player ever to do so. He entered the WSOP the following year also and he won again, netting $375,000, and becoming only the third player at the time (along with Johnny Moss and Doyle Brunson) to win poker's most prestigious tournament twice.

In the 16 years that followed his 1981 tournament win, Unger suffered through drug addiction and tumultuous wins and losses in cycles, paying off his mounting gambling debts with poker winnings only to sustain heavy losses on horse and sports wagers. In all, he won 10 major No-Limit poker titles, but ultimately the demons that haunted him left him unable to enjoy his success.

Often broke, Ungar frequently moved from hotel and motel rooms to the homes of helpful friends. At the age of 39, he entered the 1997 tournament. Incredibly, he once again won first prize, cementing his reputation as an all-time great – elevating his record to match the three Main Event championship titles held by legendary Johnny Moss. He used the $1 million to wipe away his debts once and for all.

Making the comeback of a lifetime, it seemed Ungar had been given a second chance at life, but the cards held something else in store. For many years he had battled cocaine addiction in addition to his gambling problem. Just a few months after his landmark win, he was found dead at the Oasis Motel in Las Vegas. The death was ruled accidental – a nonlethal mixture of narcotics and painkillers that had aggravated a hereditary heart condition.

By 1999, the game was exploding. Construction of the Bellagio and other new, upscale casinos attracted more poker players while providing stiff competition to the Horseshoe. The WSOP kept chugging anyway. The final table in the 2001 Main Event featured a murderer's row of Phil Hellmuth, Carlos Mortensen, Dewey Tomko, Mike Matusow and Phil Gordon, all elite, aggressive players. Their wise-cracking banter, with the stakes their highest, drew gaudy ratings for ESPN, establishing the event as exciting and TV-friendly. The 2001 all-star final table became a rarity, though, as the number of players increased so quickly that it took not only great skill but also supernatural luck to get to the end.

Chris Moneymaker provided the final boost that the WSOP – and the game itself – needed to launch into the stratosphere. Winning his way into the WSOP starting with a $40 supersatellite entry fee, the young, aptly-named accountant stormed through the tournament, knocking off wily pro Sam Farha to win a staggering $2.5 million. The World Poker Tour had brought other events to TV by then, and the meteoric rise of Internet poker sealed the deal. Suddenly, poker was everywhere. Attendance at the WSOP spiked from 512 in 2000 to more than 800 in 2003 and a mind-boggling 2,575 in 2004.

Nothing as small as a family squabble and some Binion financial troubles would stop the WSOP freight train. Harrah's bought the event from the Binions in 2004, then hired a management firm to run the Horseshoe. The 2005 WSOP would be split between the Horseshoe and the sprawling, Harrah's-owned Rio. The Rio plans to take over the whole event in 2006. Given the poker fever spreading the globe, it couldn't have picked a better time.

♥ ♣ ♦ ♠

ROBERT WILLIAMSON III ON DRINKING AT THE TABLE

Let me start by saying, if you're trying to gain an advantage by increasing your wit or intelligence by drinking at the table, you're not going to do it. It's going to impair your decision-making ability. However, there are two key elements that people overlook.

One is how other people approach playing against you. If you're drinking, people assume that your game is going to go way downhill and that you're very action-oriented. They'll change the way they play against you. Especially if you get on a roll against them. If you get on a roll, they'll get really timid. Then they'll think: Maybe I was wrong, maybe he plays better when he's drinking! They'll get intimidated against you. And the more they get intimidated, the more you can get a little brash, a little bolder, a little braver and you can take a few more shots against them. When people are afraid of you, it's usually good. When people are inspired to play well against you, it's usually bad, because that will make them want to play better.

The second reason why the drinking thing has worked well for me is that I'll often get other players to join me and their tolerance for alcohol may not be quite what mine is.

GLOSSARY

♥ ♣ ♦ ♦

POKER TERMINOLOGY
FOR THE AFICIONADO

✖ A ✖

ACTION: The term for all the betting and raising in a specific game. In any given round, the player who makes the first move is said to be starting the action.

AGGRESSIVE: Generally used to refer to a player who raises and bets much more often than he calls. A game can also be characterized as aggressive.

ALL-IN: Betting the remainder of one's chips during a hand.

ANTE: A mandatory bet that everyone at the table is required to post before each hand. Antes occur in stud games and in later rounds of tournaments.

✖ B ✖

BACKDOOR: Catching both the turn and river card to make a hand that generally a player has "backed" into. Also known as "runner-runner."

BACKDOOR DRAW: When you need both the turn and the river to complete a specific draw.

BAD BEAT: When a hand that is heavily favored loses to a significant underdog.

BELLY BUSTER: An inside straight draw.

BET: To put money into the pot first in a betting round.

BLANK: A board card that is unlikely to be of value to any player remaining in the hand.

BLIND (BLIND BET): Blinds are forced bets that must be posted before the cards are dealt. Generally the player two seats to the left of the dealer posts a "big" blind and the player one seat to the left of the dealer posts a "small" blind between one-third and two-thirds the size of the big blind.

BLUFF: When a player bets with a weak hand with the intention to get other players at the table to fold.

BOARD: All the community cards in a hold'em game.

BOAT: See *full house*.

BOTTOM PAIR: Pairing the lowest card currently on the board.

BUMP: To raise.

BURN: When the dealer discards the top card from the deck before dealing the flop, turn and river.

BUTTON: The button represents who holds the dealer position during a specific hand and therefore which players have to post the blinds. Also refers to the player who is on the button.

BUY: When a player bets and causes everyone else to fold, especially with a weak hand or as a bluff, he is "buying" the pot. Also known as "stealing" the pot.

✖ C ✖

CALL: To call is to match the current bet or raise.

CALLING STATION: A player who calls much more often than he bets or raises, especially with weak hands.

CAP: To put in the last raise permitted during a betting round in a limit game.

CHASE: To attempt to outdraw an opponent's hand that is likely better than yours now, but is worse than the hand you are chasing.

CHECK: To decline to bet.

CHECK RAISE: As a move of deception, to check and then raise after a player following you in the round bets.

COLD-CALL: If one player bets, a second player raises and a third player calls the raise, he is cold-calling the raise.

CONNECTOR: A starting hand consisting of two cards that are one rank apart.

COUNTERFEIT: When your hand is weakened by a board card. For example, if you hold A-5 and the board is A-5-9 and the turn is a 9, that has counterfeited your hand.

CRACK: When a strong hand, usually pocket aces or pocket kings, loses to a heavy preflop underdog, it has been "cracked."

CRYING CALL: A desperate call in a large pot that you have almost no hope of winning.

✖ D ✖

DEAD MONEY: Money put in the pot by players who have already folded. Also refers to weak players in general.

DOMINATION: When two players have a common card in their starting hands and one player has a higher kicker. For example, AK has AQ dominated.

DOUBLE BELLY BUSTER: See *double gutshot.*

DOUBLE GUTSHOT: When you hold two separate one-card straight draws. For example, if you hold 8-9 and the board is 6-10-Q, either a 7 or a J gives you a straight.

DRAWING DEAD: When a player tries to make a hand which, even if made, will not win the pot.

✖ E ✖

EARLY POSITION: Usually refers to the first three positions to the left of the blinds, but any time you are in a position where you must act before most of the other players in a betting round.

✖ F ✖

FAMILY POT: A pot in which most, if not all, of the players at the table call before the flop.

FIFTH STREET: The fifth and final community card, also known as the river.

FISH: A weak player who is outmatched in the current game.

FLOP: First three community cards dealt as a group in Hold'em and Omaha.

FLUSH: A hand where all five cards are of the same suit.

FLUSH DRAW: When you hold four suited cards and another card of that suit gives you a flush.

FOLD: To give up on a hand rather than call the current bet.

FOUR-FLUSH: A flush draw.

FOUR-OF-A-KIND: A hand consisting of four cards of the same rank.

FOURTH STREET: The fourth community card, also known as the turn.

FREE CARD: A card that a player gets to see without calling any bet.

FREEROLL: When two players have the same hand but only one player can improve, that player has a "freeroll."

FULL HOUSE: A hand consisting of three cards of one rank and two cards of another rank.

❊ G ❊

GUTSHOT: An inside-straight draw.

❊ H ❊

HEADS-UP: When only two players remain in a hand, they are heads-up.

HIT: A player is said to have "hit" when a card comes that completes his draw.

❊ I ❊

IMPLIED ODDS: While pot odds count only the money in the pot, implied odds also consider the future bets that could be won in comparison to the bet that must be called.

INSIDE STRAIGHT DRAW: When one rank of card will give you a straight. For example, if you hold 8-9 and the board is 5-7-x and any 6 will give you a straight.

❊ K ❊

KICKER: When one of the two cards in a pocket make a pair, the other card is called a kicker. For example if you have AK and the board is A-x-x, then your hand is a pair of aces with king kicker.

Kickers break ties when more than one player has the same top pair.

❊ L ❊

LATE POSITION: Generally refers to the button and one seat right of the button, but also any time you are in a position where you act after most of the other players in a betting round.

LAYDOWN: A player folding his hand.

LIMP: When you call a bet instead of raise.

LOOSE: A player who plays a lot of hands or a game with many players who play a lot of hands.

❊ M ❊

MANIAC: A player who bets and raises wildly with any hand in any position.

MIDDLE PAIR: Pairing a card on the board that is neither the highest nor lowest.

MIDDLE POSITION: Refers to the seats four or more to the left of the big blind and before late position.

MUCK: To fold.

MULTIWAY POT: A pot with more than two people.

❊ N ❊

NO-LIMIT: A type of poker in which a player may bet all of the chips he has during any round of betting.

NUTS: The best possible hand at that point in the hand.

❊ O ❊

OPEN-ENDED STRAIGHT DRAW: When you hold four cards in sequence and two ranks of cards will give you a straight. For example, if you hold 8-9 and the board is 10-J-x and any 7 or Q gives you a straight.

OUTS: Cards that will improve a player's current hand, usually used when a hand is likely behind and drawing to a likely winner.

OVERCALL: If one player bets, a second player calls and a third player calls, the third player has made an overcall.

OVERCARD: A card that is higher than any on the board. Also, cards that are higher than cards in your hand.

OVERPAIR: A pocket pair that is higher than any card on the board.

⌘ P ⌘

PAIR: Two cards of the same rank.

PASSIVE: A player who calls a lot and rarely raises or bets is referred to as passive.

PAY-OFF: To call a bet where you are pretty sure you are beat, but the pot is sufficiently large to justify a call anyway.

POCKET PAIR: A starting hand where both cards are of the same rank.

POT: All the money that has been bet in the hand up until that point.

POT ODDS: The amount of money in the pot compared to the amount you must put in the pot to continue playing.

PUT SOMEONE ON: When you have guessed what hand someone else holds.

⌘ Q ⌘

QUADS: Four-of-a-kind.

⌘ R ⌘

RABBIT HUNTING: Asking the dealer to see what cards would have been dealt if the hand had continued.

RAG: A card that is likely to have no consequence on the outcome of the hand.

RAGGED: A flop or board without many obvious draws.

RAINBOW: A flop where each card is of a different suit.

RAISE: To make an additional bet to whatever has already been bet in the round.

RAKE: The percentage the casino or cardroom takes from each hand.

REPRESENT: A bet a player makes to make other players think he has a certain hand.

RERAISE: To make an additional bet when the pot has already been bet and raised.

RIVER: The fifth and last community card, also known as fifth street.

ROCK: A tight, patient player.

ROYAL STRAIGHT FLUSH: An ace-high straight flush.

RUNNER-RUNNER: See *backdoor*.

RUSH: When a player wins a large number of pots in a short period of time.

⌘ S ⌘

SANDBAG: See *slow play*.

SCARE CARD: A board card that may complete an opponent's hand and make it better than your current hand.

SCOOP: To win an entire pot in a high-low game.

SEMI-BLUFF: A bet by a player who likely does not have the best hand, but has outs and may win the pot by betting.

SET: A hand consisting of three-of-a-kind with two of the rank as hole cards and the other on the board.

SHARK: A strong player who can dominate the current game.

SHORT STACK: A chip count that is small relative to the amount of chips other players have at the table.

SHOWDOWN: When more than one player is left at the end of the action, and players have to show their hands.

SIDE POT: When a player has gone all-in and other players make additional bets, those bets go into a side pot rather than the main pot.

SLOW PLAY: To play a strong hand timidly in order to entice other players to remain in the hand.

SPLIT POT: A pot that is divided equally between two players because they have equivalent hands.

STEAL: See *buy.*

STRAIGHT: A hand where all five cards are in sequential order but of different suits.

STRAIGHT FLUSH: A hand where all five cards are of the same suit and in sequential order.

SUCKER: If you don't know who this is…it's probably you.

SUITED: A starting hand where both cards are of the same suit.

SUITED CONNECTOR: A starting hand consisting of two cards that are one rank apart and of the same suit.

⭒ T ⭒

TELL: A clue a player inadvertently gives out about the strength of his hand due to certain actions or gestures.

THREE-OF-A-KIND: A hand with three cards of the same rank.

TIGHT: A player who plays very few hands and a game that features a number of players who play very few hands.

TILT: To play wildly or recklessly; a player usually goes "on tilt" after experiencing a bad beat.

TOP PAIR: Pairing the highest card currently on the board.

TRIPS: Three-of-a-kind. For Hold'em specifically, when one of your hole cards matches a pair on the board.

TURN: The fourth community card, also called fourth street.

TWO PAIR: A hand with two pairs.

⭒ U ⭒

UP: This is an expression meaning two pair. For example, aces "up" means a two-pair hand where the high pair is aces.

UNDERDOG: A hand that is less likely to win.

UNDER THE GUN: The player who must act first on a betting round.

SOME STUFF YOU MIGHT WANT TO LOOK UP

ACKNOWLEDGMENTS

First off, let me say that Pat Broderick is a genius and that without him, this book wouldn't exist. Pat is a consummate professional, a joy to work with, and a brilliantly creative guy. Many thanks also to Charlie Conrad, who provided the idea for *The Poker Aficionado*. Thanks, Charlie, for picking me from the sea of poker degenerates to execute it. Frank Scatoni and Greg Dinkin of Venture Literary have provided invaluable support and advice throughout the process, not to mention the thanks they get for opening up their Rolodex. Jeremy Katz gets special thanks for helping me craft a lifestyle where I can do the job I love and have time to work on books like this one.

Alison Presley at Random House has been a help throughout the process. Stephanie LaCroix Hinkaty did a great job proofreading. Jennifer Thornton gets credit for helping figure out how to make all this happen.

This has been a collaborative effort and I got a ton of help in doing the research and even the writing. Jonah Keri contributed a number of pieces: Hand Odds, Chip Proxies, Poker Superstitions, WSOP Main Event Winners and Prize Money, Poker Jokes, Best Places to Play Online, Best Poker Foods, Non-Poker Poker

Games, Best Poker Home Games, Best Weird, Regional or Not-as-Widely Known Home Games, Poker Games with Funny Names, Best Poker Rooms in the World, Best Las Vegas Poker Rooms, and the History of the WSOP.

Patrick Larsen is another friend who helped me out by writing the pieces on Equipment and Entering the WSOP, also the profiles of Johnny Moss and Stu Ungar.

Others who deserve credit: Matt Blankman wrote the TV section. Adam Katz and Rene Lyons did the legwork for the glossary and hand nicknames. Henry Wasserman helped out in a big way in the Poker Blogs section.

I'm also extremely grateful to all the players who've taken time out to help me: Ashley Adams, Mike Caro, Scott Fischman, Phil Gordon, Clonie Gowen, Jay Greenspan, Phil Hellmuth, Howard Lederer, Matt Lessinger, Kathy Liebert, Matt Matros, Amarillo Slim Preston, David Sklansky, John Vorhaus and Robert Williamson III.

I'd also like to thank my wife, Susan Van Metre, for all her help with the book and for always being there for me.